TWO COUNTRIES

Katrina Porteous was born in Aberdeen, grew up in Co. Durham, and has lived on the Northumberland coast since 1987. She read History at Cambridge and afterwards studied in the USA on a Harkness Fellowship. Many of the poems in her first collection, *The Lost Music* (Bloodaxe Books, 1996), focus on the Northumbrian fishing community, about which Katrina has also written in prose in *The Bonny Fisher Lad* (The People's History, 2003). Katrina also writes in Northumbrian dialect, and has recorded her long poem, *The Wund an' the Wetter*, on CD with piper Chris Ormston (Iron Press, 1999). Her second full-length collection from Bloodaxe, *Two Countries* (2014), was shortlisted for the Portico Prize for Literature in 2015.

Katrina has been involved in many collaborations with other artists, including public art for Seaham, Co. Durham, with sculptor Michael Johnson, and two books with maritime artist James Dodds, *Longshore Drift* (Jardine Press, 2005) and *The Blue Lonnen* (Jardine Press, 2007). She often performs with musicians, including Chris Ormston, Alistair Anderson and Alexis Bennett. She is particularly known for her radio-poetry, much of it produced by Julian May. One of these poems, *Horse*, with electronic music by Peter Zinovieff, first performed at Sage Gateshead for the BBC Radio 3 Free Thinking Festival 2011, is published as an artists' book and CD, with prints by Olivia Lomenech Gill (Windmillsteads Books, 2014).

Katrina's third full-length collection, *Edge* (Bloodaxe Books, 2019), draws on three collaborations commissioned for performance in Life Science Centre Planetarium, Newcastle, between 2013 and 2016, with multi-channel electronic music by Peter Zinovieff: *Field*, *Sun* and *Edge*. *Sun* was part of NUSTEM's *Imagining the Sun* project for schools and the wider public (Northumbria University, 2016). *Edge*, a poem in four moons incorporating sounds collected from space missions, was broadcast as a *Poetry Please* Special on BBC Radio 4 in 2013.

For my mother and father

KATRINA PORTEOUS

TWO COUNTRIES

BLOODAXE BOOKS

ISBN: 978 1 85224 830 7

First published 2014 by
Bloodaxe Books Ltd,
Eastburn,
South Park,
Hexham,
Northumberland NE46 1BS.

www.bloodaxebooks.com
For further information about Bloodaxe titles
please visit our website or write to
the above address for a catalogue.

Supported using public funding by
ARTS COUNCIL
ENGLAND

Cover design: Neil Astley & Pamela Robertson-Pearce

This is a digital reprint of the 2014 Bloodaxe edition.

CONTENTS

INTRODUCTION

Two Countries is a book of poems about place. By place, I mean not just land, but the people who shape it, and the conversation between them and their environment. It is also a book of a particular type of poem. For the most part, these are dramatic constructs which eschew the 'personal' element common to much contemporary poetry. Secondly, many of them are very long. Thirdly, all but two short poems in this collection are commissions: poems which I have been invited to write to a deadline on a particular subject for a distinct audience. Lastly, they have all been written to be heard rather than read. Many of them were written explicitly as 'radio-poems', and so belong to a distinct genre. All are, I believe, primarily composed of sound rather than of print, and are best understood as music.

The long poems in this book are a collage of scraps and fragments, an archaeological assemblage of speech, song, litany, chant and other forms of words. I have performed most of them many times, sometimes with accompaniment from musicians, playing instruments as diverse as Northumbrian pipes and computer-controlled electronics. Each time a long poem is performed, it is different. There is no 'definitive' version of any of these long poems; like the landscapes they represent, they are provisional. In that sense, nailing them down in a book is impossible. In the e-book version of *Two Countries*, many of the poems are simultaneously available as audio, and the audio version sometimes differs from the printed text.

Radio-poetry as a genre is a way of exploring the question: what makes listening to a poem different from listening to the News? My first attempt at radio writing came in 1998, on the BBC's Write Out Loud course, run by Sue Roberts and Simon Armitage at Lumb Bank. On it, writers were taught to use a DAT (digital audio tape) recorder, sent out to collect field recordings and to write, then each given two hours of studio time with a BBC Studio Manager to produce their own five-minute piece. I had just returned from a writing residency in Shetland, and wrote and produced a poem called *Weather Words*, about taboo words which Shetland fishermen consider unlucky. This piece used dialect, layered voices, and chants which I recorded with children from the local primary school. These were all techniques intended to make people listen to the words in a less intellectual, more abstract and sensual, way. I have gone on to develop several of these techniques in the poems in *Two Countries*.

My first national radio commission was *This Far and No Further*, a poem about Hadrian's Wall, commissioned by Tim Dee for his Radio 4 series *Up Against the Wall* in autumn 2000. Although this was almost my first radio-poem, I already had lots of experience of writing poems about place. My working practice involves three key ingredients: walking, listening and a notebook. I often carry an audio recorder as well. Maps and historical documents are also important, especially as a source of place names, which help root the poems in the actual landscape. But boots on the ground, sounds, and the voices of people who truly know a place, are the living source of these poems.

Many years ago, I was introduced to Charles Parker, Peggy Seeger and Ewan MacColl's innovative *Radio Ballads*, which are often said to have begun this kind of documentary approach. What Parker, Seeger and MacColl did so brilliantly was to reinvent for radio a much older tradition, that of the balladeer, and to mix it with real, recorded speech. When they were first broadcast in the late 1950s and early 60s, it was revolutionary to hear unscripted ordinary speech on radio. But using speech as the source for a ballad is not new at all. In fact, it is probably one of the oldest poetic traditions. I had been working in this way for years before I first heard the *Radio Ballads*. I walk, observe, listen, and make notes as I go. I interview people, and make more notes. Among these scribbles, pages and pages of them, key phrases will glint like ore. One line or phrase will resonate with another far away. Its sound and rhythm will suggest other lines. So a poem, or ballad, begins.

My research for *This Far and No Further* consisted of walking along the Wall, and talking to people involved in its care, including representatives of the National Trust and National Park. It quickly became apparent to me that, while the Roman occupation lasted less than 300 years, the land itself has been continually occupied and grazed for around 4,000 years; and that it is upon that ancient livestock farming culture that this World Heritage Site still depends. So it was the hill farming community whose views of the Wall informed this poem. My interviewees gave me such lines as: 'Aah cannot say much good about it,' and 'Butter and eggs kept the house, and the wool paid the rent.' The rest of the poem grew from such key lines.

In addition, I wrote chants composed of the names of old fields and steadings, which were performed by children from Haltwhistle First School. Intermittently throughout the poem, I layered these chants against another speaker's voice. This gives the effect of hearing the words differently, even of losing them altogether in pure sound – in this case, a martial music. I developed this method of layering voices using a primitive technique, experimenting with a pair of cassette tape recorders. I did not use computer audio-editing software while writing any of these poems, although I always wrote with it in mind, because I knew that the BBC would use a computer to produce them. Layered voices present a particular challenge in print. Wherever I have used two or more voices at once in any of the radio-poems in this book, I have laid out the text in parallel columns to indicate simultaneity.

This Far and No Further was broadcast in January 2001, a month before Britain's first outbreak of foot-and-mouth disease for over 30 years was discovered at a farm at Heddon-on-the-Wall. That episode, which lasted until October, involved the slaughter of around ten million sheep and cattle, the vast majority of them disease-free. It was a study in bureaucratic incompetence. The panic and heartbreak which ensued within the agricultural community cannot be forgotten. Just as the disease was at its height, I was commissioned by Radio 3 to write a poem for its Poetry Proms series, to be broadcast in the interval of one of the Proms concerts. With crashing irony, the theme that year was 'pastoral'. I could no longer visit my interviewees along the Wall: the countryside was in lockdown, travelling restrictions so severe, it almost felt as if we were under occupation. So I interviewed by telephone. Once again, direct speech became the ore of the poem. The sense that the country was divided, that London neither understood nor cared for what the countryside was suffering, was raw and real. *An Ill Wind* was researched and written in a fortnight. It was to be recorded in performance, so there was no opportunity to use more than one voice. I read it to a London audience in the Serpentine Pavilion that August. It was produced by Sara Davies and broadcast a few days later to considerable audience response.

The last and briefest poems in this series, one of which gives this book its title, are *Two Countries* and *The Ruined Thistles*. These were not radio-poems. They were commissioned a year later, by Arts UK, for an international project called *Writing On the Wall*, which linked places and communities along Hadrian's Wall with writers from the countries which had originally garrisoned it. These two small poems comment on the aftermath of foot-and-mouth. *Two Countries* in particular points to the increasing separation of "town" and "country" in perceptions of Englishness. The oak sapling grew because, for some time after foot-and-mouth, there were no sheep to graze the fell.

The second section of this book, *Borderers*, begins with a Wall poem, *The Ruined Thistles*, because *Wall* and *Borderers* are contiguous. The land north of the Wall running into southern Scotland is a hilly no man's land: 'Neither England nor Scotland. Itself alone.' For centuries, until the Union of the Crowns in 1603, this area was riven by conflict. Sometimes this was national in character; more often it took the form of continuous and bitter tribal warfare between feuding families, who had more in common with one another on either side of the Border than they had with their own countrymen farther afield. Before the modern Anglo-Scottish Border was drawn, the Anglo-Saxon kingdom of Northumbria stretched from the Forth to the Humber, and Border Scots and the Northumbrian dialect are still essentially the same language. Borderers, whether English or Scottish, remain in many ways one people. I wrote *Borderers*, with its chant of Border family names, in response to a commission from BBC Radio Scotland in 2002 for a UK BBC documentary series called *A Sense of Place*. The producer was Adam Fowler.

Tweed is unusual in this book, in that, although very long, it is not a radio-poem. It was commissioned in 2004 by the Tweed Rivers Interpretation Project, for an anthology of new writing and art called *Tweed Rivers*. For this project, 12 writers were paired with artists and assigned a section of river in the Tweed catchment area, with the brief to bring alive its stories. I was allotted the great river itself, and paired with sculptor and photographer Susheila Jamieson. This was a poem I had long wanted to write, for a number of reasons. First, the Tweed is one of the world's great salmon rivers, I live 25 miles from its estuary, and I had written for years about men who fished for salmon in the sea. Tensions exist between the few remaining salmon netsmen – mainly at sea, with just a handful left on the river – and the powerful angling fraternity, who have lobbied for an end to netting. Secondly, my family name, Porteous, originates from a tiny Border stronghold called Hawkshaw, now at the bottom of the Fruid Reservoir, within a mile or two of the source of the Tweed in the Moffat Hills. Thirdly, for part of its length, the Tweed forms an actual physical border between Scotland and England.

Time was short and the river long. I had only three months to research and write about over 100 miles of river. In addition, the summer of 2004 was one of the wettest anyone could remember. For two months, I squelched along as much of the Tweed as was publicly accessible (and a lot that was not). Susheila and I worked separately. I recorded interviews with shepherds, farm-managers, unemployed former mill-workers, water bailiffs, gillies, landowners in formidable castles, the last traditional salmon netsmen on the river, and a lifelong elderly poacher called Joe. Their voices all found their way into the poem, expressing the many tensions between older and contemporary ways of life, and our differing approaches to what we mean by "nature".

Dunstanburgh was written for Radio 4 in 2003. It was one of the few poems in *Two Countries* for which I sought a commission, rather than responding to an invitation. It was a poem which I had wanted to write for two decades. I live almost within sight of Dunstanburgh Castle and spent a year during my 20s visiting its ruins several times a week in all weathers, to record in minute detail its seasonal changes. I also researched its folklore, including tales of ghostly children's voices, and the story of Sir Guy the Seeker. According to this story, a knight visiting the castle is shown a girl trapped in crystal in the rock, and is given a choice between a bugle and a sword to free her. He chooses the bugle, and is then doomed to search for her forever. Although it seems that this Dunstanburgh legend did not appear in print until the early 19th century, the story itself is an old one, and might well have carried political overtones in medieval times, reflecting on a king whose failure to dispense patronage and to provide justice led to the breakdown of law and order. I drew on all these notes, historical observations and wildlife diaries for the poem.

One of the great mysteries about Dunstanburgh Castle is why it exists at all. It was used by the local community as a refuge during raids by the Scots in the 15th century; but it would appear that its purpose was more than purely defensive. It was built by Thomas, Earl of Lancaster, whose opposition to King Edward II is well known. While I was researching this poem, a team of archaeologists from English Heritage were unearthing evidence for a series of freshwater lakes, or meres, surrounding the castle. They proved beyond doubt that it was once a man-made island. Thomas of Lancaster went to considerable expense to design his castle as a massive visual reference to the Isle of Avalon, mythical home of King Arthur. This was a provocative symbol, designed to suggest that he, Thomas, had greater legitimacy to the English throne than the King himself. In a part of the country where law and order were impossible to maintain, Thomas promised alternative 'good lordship'. But his promise came to nothing. Northumberland remained lawless, and Dunstanburgh, ruined a century and a half later during the Wars of the Roses, stands as a visual reminder of Arthurian ideals which were never realised.

To write the poem, I returned to the ruined castle frequently over the course of a year, this time with my DAT machine to record what I heard: the sea, the wind, kittiwakes on the cliffs, skylarks above the in-bye field. When I write a radio-poem, recorded sound is not an added "sound effect", but an integral part of the poem: very often, its germ. The repetitive cry of the kittiwakes, for example, became the chorus of the poem's main chant. *Dunstanburgh* is structured around a year at the castle. Like most of my long poems, it is composed of a variety of voices; made up, like the place itself, of fragments, including the songs and monologues of past human inhabitants, and the older, elemental chants of the place itself. It was recorded on location, in February (it snowed), by its producer, Julian May, read by me with an actor. The chants were performed by children from Seahouses First School. As in my other radio-poems, in places I combined two, or even three, voices speaking simultaneously, to give an effect closer to music or pure sound. At these points, the voices become, like history, almost opaque. This musical effect is impossible to reproduce in print.

I have paired *Dunstanburgh* with two short poems in this section. The first is *Shanky*, a poem which was originally part of *The Blue Lonnen* sequence, and which expresses a particular English attitude to history and landscape. The second is *A Short History of Bamburgh*, a poem commissioned by Bamburgh Parish Council for their Parish Plan in 2005. Bamburgh was a royal castle, and capital of the Anglo-Saxon Kingdom of Northumbria. Dunstanburgh was deliberately, and provocatively, built within sight of it; so I have placed the two poems side by side.

The poems in the *Sea Roads* section of *Two Countries* return to a theme which I explored in my first Bloodaxe collection, *The Lost Music*: the lives, traditions and language of north Northumberland's fishing community. *The Wund an' the Wetter* began early in 1999 as a commission from Iron Press in association with the Northumbrian Language Society. The brief was for a Northumbrian dialect poem to be performed with new pipe music by Chris Ormston, at the launch of *The Northumborman*, the collected dialect poems of Fred Reed. Since the publication of *The Lost Music*, a number of my friends from the fishing villages had died, taking their language with them. I still had recordings of many of them; so I sat down with transcripts of our conversations, and assembled two lists: one containing vocabulary, words connected with fishing, weather, birds and the sea, and the other made up of idiomatic phrases from everyday speech. These phrases were exclamatory, strongly rhythmic, and mainly based on a three-beat, anapaestic metre: 'Howway doon t' the chorchyard an' ask the aa'd men!' 'By, lad, she's a reight Taggarine-man's haal!''Ye meight as weel taalk t' the man i' the moon!' 'They'd dae little for God if the divvil was deed!' and the wonderful 'Come wi' the wund an' gan wi' the wetter', meaning 'Easy come, easy go'. The rattling energy of these rhythms, together with the lists of disappearing words, dictated the poem; and although I am not, and do not pretend to sound like, a true dialect speaker, I am pleased to have captured a glimpse of a now-vanished culture.

Elsewhere in *Two Countries* I use dialect in reported speech as and when I find it. Dialect is a fluid medium; there is considerable inconsistency in its use from place to place and from speaker to speaker, and these inconsistencies are reflected here. Spelling, too, is only approximate. I have provided a glossary, the bulk of which consists of words spoken in Beadnell and collected in *The Wund an' the Wetter*.

All the other poems in the *Sea Roads* section, including the *Blue Lonnen* sequence, were written in 2006 as a commission from Alnwick Playhouse and Northumberland Coast AONB, to accompany an exhibition of photographs by Nigel Shuttleworth. All Nigel's photographs were of the traditional Northumbrian boat, the coble, a lovely, open, clinker-built vessel, with a long history. Like the Northumbrian language, it contains elements of Scandinavian, Anglo-Saxon and Celtic history. The word 'coble' appears in 14th century accounts of fishing, and I have found evidence to show continuity in fishing methods from that time well into the 20th century. So coble fishing was truly sustainable; but like much in Northumbrian culture, it has come to an end in our lifetimes, superseded by more efficient boats with more powerful engines, which cost more to run and require more intensive fishing. There are few people alive who know how to build a coble. I was helped in writing these poems by one of the finest, Hector Handyside of J. and J. Harrisons' boatyard, Amble. The disappearance of the coble marks the end, not just of a beautiful object, but of a whole network of relations between people and their environment. Whereas a modern, fibreglass boat is often operated by just one man, a coble, with a crew of three, required a whole community to maintain it. I wrote *The Blue Lonnen* sequence as an elegy to that communality of people, boat and place. 'Lonnen' is the Northumbrian word for a lane, and *The Blue Lonnen* is at once an actual path of mussel shells discarded from fishing bait, the sea itself, and the long line of tradition which it represents.

The poems in the *Coal Roads* section are the earliest in this book. They begin with a sequence called *The Dark Passages*, written in

1998 for *Book of the North*, a project devised by W.N. Herbert, in which poets, novelists and visual artists collaborated in an alternative history of the North. The aim was to produce what was at that time cutting-edge technology and now sounds like ancient history: an interactive CD-ROM. Writers were invited to contribute text which could be presented either as sound or as visual content. Inspiration came from group visits to the lead-mining landscape around Allenheads. We were also given some basic instruction in computer animation and sound-editing programmes. As usual, my imagination ran ahead of my pitiful technical ability: I wanted to replicate the sedimentary geology of the Pennine landscape in a series of "layered" poems, which could be visually "excavated" by the reader. But I had barely begun to get to grips with a computer. Artist Alan Smith incorporated lines from *The Dark Passages* into animations on the CD-ROM, which was published by New Writing North in 2000. *The Dark Passages* was also set to music by the late Keith Morris, as part of *Songs from the Drowned Book*, a sequence which included poems by Sean O' Brien and W.N. Herbert, and which was performed at Newcastle BigFest in July 1999.

The rest of the poems in this section originated in a multi-agency project called *Turning the Tide*, which took place between 1996 and 2000, and consisted of a £10 million programme to remove 1.3 million tonnes of former colliery waste from the so-called 'Black Beaches' of East Durham. I was commissioned by Easington District Council in 1999, first to collect stories from the communities of Seaham, Easington Colliery and Blackhall; then to provide lines for bronze sculptures and plaques by Michael Johnson at Seaham; then to contribute information for interpretation panels along the new coastal footpath. Easington Colliery Parish Council separately commissioned me to write an inscription for the Colliery Memorial Garden. Finally, I was asked to write poetry for an exhibition which brought together the work of two visual artists who had recorded the project, photographer Keith Pattison and painter Robert Soden. I went on to assist in editing the book of that exhibition, *Turning the Tide*, working alongside its designer, Edward Gainford.

The poem sequence grew out of my personal connection with East Durham: my mother was born there and I still had family ties to the area. I wanted to explore the contradictions which I found in the landscape and its communities, before and after the pit closures and the clean-up of the beaches. I was struck by the contrast between the darkness and violence of coal extraction and the softness and beauty of the visible Durham landscape, the pre-industrial past which surrounded the pit villages. It is easy to understand why

14

miners loved their gardens and pigeons. Secondly, I wanted to explore contradictions within the mining communities themselves: the enormous pride and solidarity in the industry; the anger and bereavement at the closure of the pits; alongside the paradoxical conviction felt by many, when the pits were still open, that they did not want their sons to work there. Thirdly, I wanted to examine the contradiction at the very heart of coal extraction: that winning coal is hugely destructive to nature, but that it confronts us forcibly with the elemental processes of creation itself. Faced with the stratified cliffs of man-made pit waste deposited on the beaches, I reflected on the igneous and sedimentary processes from which the earth is made, before which we are all equally insignificant.

Turning the Tide did a tremendous job in cleaning up the Durham beaches. At the same time, I felt strongly that I wanted to give a platform to the voices of the people I interviewed, and not allow the memory of the pits to be tidied away along with the slurry. These memories are often painful: they include not only the black beaches, but hardship, deprivation, illness, disaster, the long fight for better conditions and pay, and the bitterness of the 1984-85 strike and subsequent pit closures. A decade and a half after I wrote these poems, the former mining communities of East Durham still struggle to find a way forward. In the book *Turning the Tide*, it was not my poems but the quotations which I selected from real life interviewees which spoke most eloquently of these things.

The title of the last section of *Two Countries*, *Haliwerfolk*, is the Old English designation of the 'people of St Cuthbert'; those who held land by virtue of defending the Saint's remains and territory. Later, the term referred to Durham County and 'County Palatine': those parts of Northumberland which, until the 19th century, fell under the jurisdiction of the Bishop of Durham – particularly Holy Island and the Bamburgh coast.

Durham Cathedral is a reworking of a poem commissioned by Radio 4's *Front Row* for the first Durham *Lumiere* festival in November 2009. *Lumiere*, brought together by the arts events organisation Artichoke, was a massive son-et-lumière festival, which took place across Durham City over four nights. I loved it, its juxtaposition of the town's historic beauty and grandeur with cutting-edge computer-controlled technology; and I was particularly moved by the projection of pages from the Lindisfarne Gospels across the exterior of Durham Cathedral. It was a reminder of Durham's origins in the simplicity of Holy Island's grass and sky. I wanted my poem to allude to Durham's more recent history, too: its coal-mining past. This reworked version of the poem, without the *Lumiere* references, digs down through the geological strata of Durham's culture, to the illuminations of the Lindisfarne Gospels and words from local speech, with their Anglo-Saxon roots.

Beach Ride was another early Radio 4 commission. In 2001 I was invited by the then Poet Laureate, Andrew Motion, and producer Julian May, to contribute a one-minute poem to a series for National Poetry Day on the theme of 'Journeys'. Each poem was to be recorded by the poet on location. At that time I occasionally rode a horse from a local riding stables on the beach between Seahouses and Bamburgh. There was always a thrilling gallop home. On one occasion I took my DAT recorder with me, and recorded the sound of hooves on the sand as we galloped. Then I wrote a chant in the rhythm of those hooves. The galloping triple beat suggested Northumbrian dialect; and the resulting chant recalls the movement of time and season, with a reference to the 'spuggie', or sparrow, whose flight through a lighted hall, in a speech recorded in St Bede's *History of the English Church and People*, represents the span of a human life. As a counterpoint to this strongly-stressed chant, I wrote a softer two-beat incantation, to imitate the sound of the sea. Then, playing both chants back on an old cassette recorder, I experimented with the lines of a third, narrative, strand, until I had something which sounded right. I produced a version of the piece myself with help from a sound engineer at Clara Vale Studios, and sent it as an audio file to Julian May, who polished it for broadcast.

When the Tide Comes In was a sketch for a longer radio piece. In 2006 Julian May and I submitted an idea to Radio 3's *Between the Ears*, for what was to become *The Refuge Box*, a poem set on the tidal causeway between Holy Island and the mainland. Just before the idea was accepted I had signed up for an Arvon course at Totleigh Barton, led by radio producers Piers Plowright and Matt Thompson. Unlike *Write Out Loud*, this was not a studio-orientated course. But it did give me the opportunity to write and (with other students) perform and record this short, satirical piece, about the dangers of Holy Island causeway. I subsequently re-recorded it with friends for broadcast on the Newcastle community radio station NE1 FM.

Of the shorter poems in this section, *Horizon* was commissioned in 2000 for the Seahouses millennium video, *Village by the Sea*, made by Studio Arts TV for Seahouses Development Trust. The video was a portrait of the village, edited down from a hundred hours of interviews, for many of which I was the interviewer. The poem was my response to the turn of the millennium. Of the other three short poems, *Holy Island Arch* is the earliest, and one of only two in *Two Countries* which was not commissioned, the other being *The Whale*. I have included these poems, and *Windmill Steads* (part of *The Blue Lonnen* sequence), because I think that they resonate with the last poem in the collection, *The Refuge Box*. *Holy Island Arch* also mirrors *Durham Cathedral*, as Durham was the 'Mother House' for Holy Island Priory.

The Refuge Box was written in 2007 in response to the Radio 3 commission mentioned above. The poem focuses on a wooden cabin on stilts, half way between Holy Island and the mainland, where careless drivers who do not heed the tide-tables are obliged to take shelter to avoid being drowned. Its wider theme is the idea of sanctuary itself. Holy Island was a sanctuary for early Christian settlers; yet also a place where they faced danger and despoilation. Similarly, for migrating birds, it is both a place of refuge, and of exposure.

Like many of my poems, *The Refuge Box* grew partly out of interviews and partly out of observation and field recordings. My interviewees, whom I recorded myself, included island fishermen who remembered rescues and tragedies, a coastguard, a lifeboatman, a bird warden, a wildfowler, and the Franciscan vicar of the Island. Local fishermen provided me with the lines about bad weather signs which make up the chant which begins: 'Cobwebs doon the lonnen'. They also gave me some of the most striking images of the poem. One fisherman recalled finding the body of a drowned woman when he was a boy: 'I could remember that hand as if it was yesterday. It was pure white, Katrina... I can see them fingernails yet.' That image of the hand recurs several times in *The Refuge Box*. The idea is that such tropes should help the listener to hear the whole – the interview excerpts as much as the verse – as one piece, a poem unfolding from a multiplicity of centres.

Recurring sounds can also be used to unify a radio-poem. By far the best of these were provided for *The Refuge Box* by wildlife sound recordist, Chris Watson. In addition, I used some of my own rough field recordings, including sounds of wind and sea, geese, wigeon, waders, swan wings and sudden jet-fighters sweeping in from nowhere. Of all the sounds which carry across the great open spaces of Holy Island sands, the most characteristic is the 'singing' of grey seals, a ghostly, drawn-out, mournful 'Ooooo!' which seems both human and otherworldly. The ambiguities of this sound fascinated me, suggesting the theme of equivocation which underlies the whole poem. It seemed the aural equivalent of the reflection of the blue sky in the wet sand, the uncertainty of where land and water begin and end, the edge between what is human and what is not. So much of the poem is anchored in this seal sound and its word equivalents. In particular, the words 'blue', 'human', and the repeated question 'Who?' resonate with it, creating a kind of rhyme between the human music of speech and the in-human, disembodied sounds of the place.

Like *Dunstanburgh*, *The Refuge Box* was recorded on location and produced by Julian May. The text reproduced here is longer than the broadcast version. It brings together the voices of all the people I interviewed, including the wildfowler, whose knowledge and respect for the Island's birds reflects the contradictions between traditional and more modern attitudes to nature and conservation. At the same time, the text lacks key elements of the radio-poem. In particular, in the broadcast version, perhaps as a nod to the *Radio Ballads*, Julian and I worked together to weave excerpts from the original interviews back into the text which they had inspired. Julian also added one last voice, that of a refugee who had fled her West African homeland to seek sanctuary in England. She was an inspired addition. Like the birds which had travelled half way round the world to the Island, her voice lifts the poem from the local to the universal.

I hope that, in some sense, all the poems in *Two Countries* reson-ate beyond the local. This book does not pretend to represent North-East England or the Anglo-Scottish Borders in any way: it does not contain any poems about Newcastle, for example, or other urban voices. It is simply a gathering together of some quite disparate work, a selection from a varied and uneven output, all of it concerned with human culture, nature and the interaction between the two. I have included almost no uncommissioned work, and have excluded any work which is not about place. Neither have I included the text of radio-poems such as *Longshore Drift*, *Late Blackbird* or, more recently, *Horse* (2011) or *Edge* (2013), which are not about North-East England or the Borders. All these other poems are for a future collection.

KATRINA PORTEOUS
2014

1

WALL

Two Countries

This is the oak tree that should not be here.
It stretched its blind shoot from the ungrazed fell last year.
In the spring of no lambs, it fixed its grip on Bradley's,

Snaking pale roots through the soil, a volunteer
To fortune on the bare hill. When it grows tall
And crazed with age, the hiker on the Wall

Above the farm will pass, oblivious
As now to what it means – this doubtful peace,
This border drawn between two warring countries.

This Far and No Further

From Cawfield to Winshields,
From Thorny Doors and Bogle Hole,
From Peel Crags and Steel Rigg,
Aa' the way to Sooin' Shields.

Blow, wind,
Splinter, crack,
Snap the spine
Of the rock.
Bring rain,
Drive snow,
Ice, winter –
Wind, blow.

From Hoond Hill
To High Shields,
From Hotbank
To Hoosesteeds,
From Cuddy's Craig
To Clew Hill,
Aa' the way
To Sooin' Shields.

From Cowburn Rigg and Cawburnshield,
From Close-a-Burns and Crindledykes,
From Bonnyrigg and Beggar Bog,
Aa' the way to Sooin' Shields.

I am the King of all you see,
The sky-wide, the slant country.

Frozen breakers of bare rock
Bow before me, splinter, crack;

Black wounds where the earth bled
Intractable matter. Peat, mud,
Water closes upon its dead.

The Cow Burn,
The Knag Burn,
The Brackie Burn,
The Bean Burn,
Crag Lough,
Broomlee,
Greenlee
And Grindon.

The rush, the bent-grass and the seg,
The crippled hawthorn on the crag,

The Lang Field, the Hen Field,
The Back Fell, Seat-Side...

The hawk, the crow, the fox, the hare –
All my creatures prick with fear.

I drive the clouds, the light that picks
Shadows out among the rocks.

I heft the sheep upon the hill,
The days across the empty fell.

By night, a riveted shield of stars
Arches above my dark land, scarred
By sediments of hope and care,

Stony marks that human hands
Have written, lightly, on the land.
They go. I stay. I am the wind.

From Cowburn Rigg and Cawburnshield,
From Close-a-Burns and Crindledykes,
From Bonnyrigg and Beggar Bog,
Aa' the way to Sooin' Shields.

The quad-bike bumps
Over boulders, thumps;
Over fox-hole and cord-rig it tears,
The shepherd, a sack
Of feed on the back
And a thousand yowes in his care.

Through glaur and burn
The big tyres churn
As he flies across the fell.
Through the roar of gears
He scarcely hears
The story that each stone tells:

The tall stone of the wicket-post,
The blackened stone of the hearth,
The silent stones of the burial-place
With their secretive, circular marks,

Their meanings lost
Like a memory passed
In whispers down the days,
Round the dancing flames
When the strangers came,
In the ashes when they marched away.

From Hoond Hill
To High Shields,
From Hotbank to Hoosesteeds,
From Cuddy's Craig
To Clew Hill,
Aa' the way to Sooin' Shields.

The Lang Field,
The Hen Field,
The Back Fell,
Seat-Sides,
The Bull Park,
The Lake Field,
The White Bank,
Brocky.

There's many a place aboot the countryside
Where a farmer is master ower aal;
But here, the land decides what ye can dae wi' it:
The land's the boss alang the Waal.

For it's never gonna be barley land
And it's never gonna be bagie land.
There's nowt but yowes and galloway cows
And rashers alang the Waal.

Above Crag Lough the wild geese cry,
And scribble their signature over the sky.

A flock of lapwings flips like a tide,
Summer to winter, black to white.

Hidden in reeds, the water-rail
Screeches like a barrow with a stiff, dry wheel,

And the rook on the Wall is a soldier, bored;
His claws are wire, his beak a blade;

On the ruck of the wind he is blown awry.
The brown hare sneaks from the bracken. High

On bleak Queen's Crag, a tall stone stands,
Battle-scarred, scored by forgotten hands
From the unwritten histories of the land:

23

Four-thousand tuppings and four-thousand lambings,   *The Cow Burn, the Knag Burn,*
A million nights of the stars' reckonings.   *The Brackie Burn, the Bean Burn,*
                                                           Craig Lough, Broomlee,
Its finger stabs at the streaming sky.   *Greenlee and Grindon.*
Into the distance the wild geese fly,   *The Lang Field, the Hen Field,*
                                              The Back Fell, Seat-Side,
Scrawling inscriptions of summer passed   *The Bull Park, the Lake Field,*
While the grass goes over from green to rust   *The White Bank, Brocky.*

And the long wind keens, and the squat trees bow:

Who does the land belong to now?

I, the Wall,
Defend this place.
Across a dizziness
Of space
I am control:
A ruled line,
Mark of the safe,
The sure, the known.
I am the edge –
The frontier.
This is where the world ends:

Here.

Cliff-edge
Hawk-ledge
Fox-ladder
Adder-bed
Thorn-snag
Wind-rip
Rock-ruckle
Rook-castle
Sheep-slip
Stone-dip.
Deep drop.

Full stop.

Butter and eggs kept the house
And the wool paid the rent.
So we were warmed and fed
When pay was scant.

How many lambings passed
Since a bairn hungered?
Scarcely a living soul
Left who remembers.

And now the sheep worth nowt,
And the house to sell.
A hand that's never lambed a yowe
On Grindon Fell,

That's never once led muck from the byre
Or milked a cow,
Mouths from his soft armchair: 'Them things
Don't matter now.'

The King's Crag,
The Queen's Crag,
The Black Dyke,
The Fozy Moss,
The Cow Field,
The Pit Field,
The King's Wicket,
Caa'd Knuckles.

The jagged scrapyard of hawthorn,
A rush of wind in its hooks,
Berries ablaze like a lantern,
A robin among its roots:

The sons of ancient hedges
Bow to the east. Below,
Sky pools in the vallum.
The fields of the south glow,

Burnished copper. The north
Is verdigris and rust.
The wind harrows the silent
Lough. Violent, possessed,

Unpossessable country;
It stretches away
Into the distance, free-fall.
The rowan clings to the scree.

Neither England nor Scotland,
Itself alone:
Acres of secrets. Mouths
Stopped with a rubble of stones.

Twist and writhe   *The Cow Burn, the Knag Burn,*
And snake and stretch   *The Brackie Burn,*
Up rig and spine,   *The Bean Burn,*
Through slack and ditch;   *Craig Lough,*
The Wall goes under   *Broomlee, Greenlee*
Like a stitch.   *And Grindon.*

'Are ye dykin' it or capin' it, Davey?'
In the dip where the highroad falls
Into the vallum at Sewingshields
Two mend a wall;

Trying them this way, then that way, then this way,
Under a cold Northumbrian sky –
Dyke-stone, middle-stone, thruff-stone: drystone.
'Ye need a true eye,

Fatther used to say; and Aah can alwess mind it,
A good waaller never picks a stoene up twice.
Aye, an' there's a place for every stoene, if ye can finnd it.
Nivvor leave a space.'

Trying them this way, then that way, then this way,
A long time looking for the right stone. Bend
Your body to the rhythm of the wall and follow it;
Weight of the shoulder, eye, hand.

'The mowldie's a good hand at knockin' a dyke doon;
Soft, wet groond to the norrard, an' aal;
Frost in the joints; straight joints and watter.'
Time and forgetting will make them fall,

Trying them this way, then that way, then this way,
Brian and David, a stone at a time,
Bring a rough music to the jumble of boulders around them –
Make the stones rhyme.

Who says   *From Cawfield*
The world ends here?   *To Winshields,*
Who brings   *From Thorny Doors*
Peace and safety?   *And Bogle Hole,*
Who wields   *From Peel Crags*
The two-edged sword?   *And Steel Rigg,*
It's this far and no further now.   *Aa' the way to Sooin' Shields.*

Who owns the past?   *From Hoond Hill*
That spring,   *To High Shields,*
The stream that bears   *From Hotbank*
The money in.   *To Hoosesteeds,*
It's a fine line,   *From Cuddy's Craig*
It's a thin wall   *To Clew Hill,*
That says: This far   *Aa' the way*
And no further now.   *To Sooin' Shields.*

It's a Tourist Trail,   *From Cowburn Rigg*
It's a working farm,   *And Cawburnshield,*
It's a battleground,   *From Close-a-Burns*
It's a place to live,   *And Crindledykes,*
Where each man kills   *From Bonnyrigg*
The thing he loves   *And Beggar Bog,*
And Leisure's   *Aa' the way*
Where the money is.   *To Sooin' Shields.*

And it's this far and no further.
It's a balancing act for the future.
It's the Park and the Trust and the farmer
Who keep things just the way they are.

And it's more sheep and fewer men,
And it's more paperwork to plough through;
And it's more moor and it's fewer farms,
And it's more authorities to bow to.

It's a wet night, it's a foul night,
When the wind cracks and the rain rattles
The stones of the Wall and the sores of the heart,
It's a night for the fire and the whisky-bottle...

In the Milecastle Inn they are talking prices:
'Fower poond-twenty a yowe, and a poond expenses!'
'When mine went to mart, Aah come away wi' a bill!
Ye can guess where the next lot ended up – In a hole
Wi' a bullet between the ears. D' ye think Aah'm daft?
Whae, Aah ha' t' be, t' be farmin' alang the Waal...'

It's a black-dark back-end night. There are lights on the hill.
Out there, young Willie's cutting silage still
Over the bones of a dead Roman, in the rain.
Snug in the firelight, Willie of Edge's Green,
Rowley, Davey, Graham, Nick – the same
Fire-red faces, gutturals and names
As when Haltwhistle burned, a sheet of flames.

The Romans came
Like a bunch of thieves,
Boned our land
Like a side of beef,
Built their camps
Where our steadings lay:
It's the Romans get the plenty and the farmer pays.

They split our shielings
As ye'd paunch a hare;
When ye cross at the wicket
They grab their share.
They hammer out rules
And we obey:
It's the Romans get the plenty and the farmer pays.

Now regulations
Grow thick as weeds
And nobody asked us
And nobody agrees;
But when in Rome
It's the Roman way –
It's the Romans get the plenty and the farmer pays.

And it's more paper and less sense,   *From Cowburn Rigg and Cawburnshield,*
And it's more bureaucracy to plough through; *From Close-a-Burns and Crindledykes,*
And it's more moor and it's fewer farms,   *From Bonnyrigg and Beggar Bog,*
And it's more authorities to bow to.   *Aa' the way to Sooin' Shields.*

Once Brewed,
Twice Brewed,
Stell Green
And Bradley's;
Hawkside,
Crow Crag,
Milking Gap
And Ridley's.

Out in the dark, backs to the rain,
On Ridley Common, Bradley Green,

At Cawfields, Winshields, in the slack
Of Melkridge Common, Milking Gap,

The sheep lie down. Between them strides
The unnegotiable divide.

The same rain blows on either side.

It was the Powers-That-Be decided it:
The subsidies. Dependency. The sheep an' cows
Went on the same as ever, but control had shifted.
Aye, hinny. It's a different country now.

Aah rode a pony to the school at Hindley Steel.
Bairns waalked there from Scotchcoulthard through the benty groond.
Aah wadn't want them days a hunger back again.
Aye, hinny. But they're comin' tae us now.

Aah still can smell the hay-pikes, hear the horses'
Slow hooves doon the lonnen. Then the tractors came.
Wha wad a thowt the world wad shrink sae quickly?
Aye, hinny, but Aah've seen a deal a change.

Ye can churn an' churn aal day, an' the butter's no comin'.
Ye can try an' change, but this land winna bend nor bow.
Ye can watch the fell we fought for gan tae wilderness.
Aye, hinny. An' that's what's comin' now.

Who won this land and carved it?
Loved it, cursed it, marked it?
Who's reached the end of the safe and the known?
Whose powers do we fear to harm it?
We cared for the fell. The fell kept us.
Now they're paying us not to farm it.

And the wind bowls out of the darkness, *From Cawfield to Winshields,*
And it sings of change and sameness; *From Thorny Doors and Bogle Hole,*
From Cawfield Rig to Sewingshields Crag *From Peel Crags and Steel Rigg,*
It can find no rest, no stillness, *Aa' the way to Sooin' Shields.*

For the laws of the dark are the ways of the heart,
Of the crow, of the claws   *From Cowburn Rigg and*
  on the fox and the hawk –   *Cawburnshield,*
It's the line of the tide   *From Close-a-Burns and*
  in the sand we're writing – *Crindledykes,*
It's the slant of the land,   *From Bonnyrigg and*
  it's the slope of the age,   *Beggar Bog,*
It's the rain and the cold   *Aa' the way*
  and the wind we're fighting. *to Sooin' Shields.*

And it's no the stone but the waal, *The Cow Burn, the Knag Burn,*
And it's no the day but the life *The Brackie Burn, the Bean Burn,*
And it's no the word but the tale that ye tell: *Craig Lough, Broomlee,*
Go ask the farmer's wife.   *Greenlee and Grindon;*

For it's no the stone but the waal, *The Lang Field, the Hen Field,*
And it's no the rain but the burn; *The Back Fell, Seat-Side,*
Marry the farmer, ye marry the farm, *The Bull Park, the Lake Field,*
And ye make your bed for life. *The White Bank, Brocky;*

And it's no the word but the tale,
And it's no the day but the life,
And it's no the stone but the strength of the waal:
Go ask the farmer's wife.

The Wall's fine line divides our land.
It cuts across it like a knife,
A stony scar that will not mend.
Aah cannot say much good about it.

Aah cannot say much good about it.
Memory's short and regulations
Tie our hands and test our patience –
It's a fine line between staying and leaving.

It's a fine line between staying and leaving
When a beast sickens on a dark morning.
On the sweet fell at the spring calving
It's a fine line between hate and loving.

It's a fine line between hate and loving.
Aah cannot say much good about it.
When he's out at the yowes with the snaa' blawin'
It's a fine line, living, dying.

It's a fine line, dying, living.
From the stone on the fell to the stone in the steading,
It's a fine line between staying and leaving.
It's a fine line between hate and loving.

From Cawfield to Winshields,
From Thorny Doors and Bogle Hole,
From Peel Crags and Steel Rigg,
Aa' the way to Sooin' Shields.

High on its crag, the Wall glares down
On moss and moor, on track and stone;

On lintel, hearth and cairn; all marks
Invisible beneath the dark.

The last light burning on the hill
At Hotbank Farm snaps out. The fell

And miles of scarp stretch black and blind,
And there is no voice but the wind:

I wear men down like stones. They pass
Into the dark, no more, no less
Than wave on wave through the long grass.

Once Brewed,
Twice Brewed,
Stell Green
And Bradley's;
Hawkside,
Crow Crag,
Milking Gap
And Ridley's;

From Cawfield
To Winshields,
From Thorny Doors
And Bogle Hole,
From Peel Crags
And Steel Rigg,
Aa' the way
To Sooin' Shields.

The King's Crag,
The Queen's Crag,
The Black Dyke,
The Fozy Moss,
The Cow Field,
The Pit Field,
The King's Wicket,
Caa'd Knuckles.

From Cawfield to Winshields,
From Thorny Doors and Bogle Hole,
From Peel Crags and Steel Rigg,
Aa' the way to Sooin' Shields;

From Hoond Hill to High Shields,
From Hotbank to Hoosesteeds,
From Cuddy's Craig to Clew Hill,
Aa' the way to Sooin' Shields.

Blow, wind,
Splinter, crack,
Snap the spine
Of the rock.
Bring rain,
Drive snow,
Ice, winter –
Wind, blow.

From Cowburn Rigg
And Cawburnshield,
From Close-a-Burns
And Crindledykes,
From Bonnyrigg
And Beggar Bog,
Aa' the way
To Sooin' Shields.

An Ill Wind

Hiss of the breeze in the high horse-chestnut
Over the yard;
Over the worn stones of the hemmel,
Not a word.

No sharp-pricked prints by the drinking trough.
No muck. No stink. The flies
Wash their hands on the thistle-tops;
And the breeze

Ruffles the feathery grass that grows
Too tall.
A shock of yellow ragwort choking the gate
Tells all.

It's a long, long way from the capital to the Seven Acre Field,
And it's too far to shout,
It's too far to say
And it's getting farther every day,
  And the knackerman,
  Aye, the knackerman,
  The knackerman's in the cattleshed now.

Say we're lost in a forest of paper – drowned in a river of ink,
Trapped like a ewe in a fathom of snow,
With a licence to come
And a licence to go,
And tomorrow a licence to think;
But it's too far to shout,
It's too far to say
And it's getting farther every day,
  And the knackerman,
  Aye, the knackerman,
  The knackerman's in the cattleshed now.

'There's plenty'll ride on the back a this trouble,'
Says Jack a' the Garage. 'Aye, if th' could,
Wi' sheep th' canna move nor sell, they'd be better off hevin' it.
It's an ill wund blaa's naebody good.'

33

'I don't know what all the fuss is about,' says Jenny from Telesales.
'They'd be killing them anyway in the end. The tears are a sham;
Quite hypocritical, really.' 'Aye,' says the wind in the heather,
'But yowes full a lambs…'

'Whae, there's a time for aal things,' says old man Robson
To his grizzled collie. 'We're finished, lad, an' that's a fact:
Aah'd sooner hev a lifetime a debt on me doorstep
An' me cattle back.'

Whae, Aah'm tellin' ye noo, though ye might no believe me,
Whether it's age, noo Aah'm varnigh seventy,
This has been warse than a deeth in the family:
The knackerman's in the cattleshed now.

First they shut the slaughterhouse and the little, local marts;
The sheep and the cattle will have to travel,
It's a long way,
It's a hard way,
And it's too far to shout,
It's too hard to say
And it's getting harder every day
When you're all ravelled up in the paperchase,
So you'd better shut your eyes and pray
It's a long road from the subsidy
To signing the last of your freedom away.
It's a long, long road from the cattleshed to what the nation's papers say;
But it's close as a kiss to the capital,
And it's getting closer every day,
    And the knackerman,
    Aye, the knackerman,
    The knackerman's in the cattleshed now.

Hiss of the breeze in the high horse-chestnut
Over dead ground;
Beneath the looming, windowless bastle,
Not a sound.

Between the cobbles, scraped like dinner-plates
Scrubbed clean,
Not a hair, not a straw, not a speck of muck.
The reivers have been.

The reivers have been and taken our sheep and cattle
And tied our hands,
And the brambles ravel like wires, and the fells blacken
To No Man's Land.

Once they capped the colliery shaft, it was goodbye ships and steel,
And it all seemed far from the cattle-mart and the Seven Acre Field;
Then the fishing fleet burned on the beach and it's farewell all our boats:
And now it's the power to feed ourselves that's going up in flames and smoke.
And it's too far to shout,
It's too far to say
And it's getting farther every day,
   For the knackerman,
   Aye, the knackerman,
   The knackerman's in the cattleshed now.

Whisht
Grass,
Sigh
Soft;
Far
Hills,
Hush,
Hush.

   The knackerman,
   Aye, the knackerman.

Farm,
Field,
Sky,
Fell,
Whisht,
Whisht,
Sigh
Soft.

   The knackerman.

Swish
Grass,
Sun,
Sift;

Wash
Rain,
Wind,
Whisht.

Hush.

Hush.

These are the seven silences of a black season:
First, all movement frozen. Shut down
The invisible machinery of the countryside – the hunt, the patter,
The auctioneer's song.

Next comes the silence you wait for the telephone to shatter.
You can't sleep. Can't eat. The silence of fear
Crackles like electricity down the wires; and the silence of paper
Drifts like snow through the door.

Such a queer thing to tell in sheep: a lamb a bit 'hangy'
Or a ewe that will not come to the trough.
Ice-sharp, the silence after the vet has given his verdict.
This is the silence of disbelief.

The next silence is the worst silence. This is the silence
Of the steaming kitchen at three a.m.
When half the cattle lie stiff in the yard and half are still waiting.
This is a silence with no name.

The sixth silence is the silence of grass growing,
Oceans of grass that hush, hush in the wind.
It is hard to get used to this silence: grass growing, and questions
Swelling like streams underground.

And what will you do with all the questions? When a whisper, a rush, a torrent
Bursts from the farmyard into Whitehall, what will you get?
Nothing but frozen faces, and the last silence:
A barred gate.

And it's a long way from Westminster to the cattle at the wagon-gate,
And it's a long way from the heather hill to the gravy on your plate;
It's a long, long way from the gaucho's pay,
It's more than half the world away,

When he's only earning a quid a day,
And that's the meat
That you
Just ate:
For it's too far to shout,
It's too hard to say
And it's getting harder every day,
  And the knackerman,
  Aye, the knackerman,
  The knackerman's in the cattleshed now,
  The knackerman's in the cattleshed, now.

2

BORDERERS

The Ruined Thistles

Have loosened their armour.
Their sweat-blackened leather

And tarnished spikes
Shrink, the phalanx

Of glinting weapons,
Disarrayed, softens.

They are losing the fight,
The struggle to stay upright.

Old drunks, their wits
Fly-blown, sour as piss,

They scrabble with dirty nails,
Droop grey heads, spill

Themselves, a filthy
Straggle, and loll

About, their flies undone.
They have turned themselves inside out.

A breeze rustles their hair,
Soothes them. It is the law:

Lambs fatten. Oats
Ripen. Virtue rots

From the inside. Reason
Has finally burst them open.

Their wits fly away like smoke
Into next year, and next.

Borderers

(Whispered, menacing)
Are ye one of us?
Are ye for us or agin us?
Are ye one of us?
Are ye for us or agin us?
Are ye one of us?
Are ye for us or agin us?
Are ye for us or agin us?
Are ye one of us?

Are ye Armstrong, are ye Johnstone,   *Are ye one of us?*
Are ye Hall or Reed or Heron,   *Are ye for us or agin us?*
Are ye Henderson or Graham,   *Are ye one of us?*
Are ye Beattie, Bell or Potts,   *Are ye for us or agin us?*
Are ye Musgrave, are ye Dixon,   *Are ye one of us?*
Are ye Widderington or Nixon,   *Are ye for us or agin us?*
Are ye Charlton, are ye Robson,   *Are ye for us or agin us?*
Are ye wi' us, or ye not?   *Are ye one of us?*

Wool on the whin's barb marks the track.

The violence of molten rock
Stretches before you like the sea.

From Eildon's summit you look out
On frozen time. For miles, the black

Impenetrable, speechless hills
Of Liddesdale and Teviotdale,

Redesdale, Coquetdale, North Tyne –
Rucked and buckled, patched with pine,

Cold, embattled, acid-green
Moorland, blackland, carved between
Floes of ice and tides of men,

Fastnesses of bracken, slopes
And gullies – fold their secrets close,

While the searchlight of the sun
Sweeps across them, one by one.

Are ye one of us?
Are ye for us or agin us?
Are ye one of us?
Are ye for us or agin us?
(Fade down)

Three things have no end:
Fear, hunger and the wind.

They blast the open heathland where
A single strand of wire runs.
Such a fine thread holds the peace.

Bold, defiant in the east,
At Sweethope Crag, a tower bursts
Out of bare rock, a brandished fist,

The only still, straight edge in sight.
While ragged flags of cloud and light

Tear like promises, it keeps
Its stony word upon the hill,

Unmoved, untouched, unblinking eye –
Outstares the armies of the sky,
Time its only enemy.

Are ye one of us?
Are ye for us or agin us?
Are ye for us or agin us?
Are ye one of us?
(Fade down)

Yarrow Water, Ettrick, Tweed:
A ruckle of stones and a nettle-bed,

Grey-boned hawthorn, flecked with blood,
Almost turned itself to stone,

Lichened trunk and strangled root,
Braid their shadows by the burn

In the places they belong.
Stone and tree-root: make us strong

Where the wind blows on the fell,
Where the track runs up the hill.

Who cares where you came from now?
Every ditch and fold and knowe

And the white grass that swallows down
Arrow-head and carved stone,

Becomes a place to watch and hide.
The wide land bristles, sharp with eyes.

Are ye Elliott or Maxwell,   *Are ye one of us?*
Are ye Milburn, Tait or Turnbull,   *Are ye for us or agin us?*
Are ye Rutherford or Pringle,   *Are ye one of us?*
Are ye friend or are ye foe?   *Are ye for us or agin us?*
Are ye Kerr or Hume or Little,   *Are ye one of us?*
Are ye Laidler or Liddle,   *Are ye for us or agin us?*
Are ye Storey, are ye Ridley,   *Are ye for us or agin us?*
Are ye one of us or no?   *Are ye one of us?*

Are ye Dodd or are ye Trotter,   *Are ye one of us?*
Are ye Selby, Gray or Forster,   *Are ye for us or agin us?*
Are ye Davison or Pringle,   *Are ye one of us?*
Are ye Collingwood or Scott,   *Are ye for us or agin us?*
Are ye Douglas, are ye Dixon,   *Are ye one of us?*
Are ye Heatherington or Nixon,   *Are ye for us or agin us?*
Are ye Charlton, are ye Robson,   *Are ye for us or agin us?*
Are ye wi' us, or ye not?   *Are ye one of us?*

Where Tweed and Teviot's waters meet,
They carry all away: the gates,

The fences, signposts. Pine trees sway
Like ships at mooring on their slopes.

Tree-root, picket, branch, black loam –
The flood unfastens all; its broom

Sweeps the living and the dead
Towards a place that has no borders.

South and north, the colours drain
From drowned fields as night falls

On far, unfathomable hills
That sink their differences in sleep;

One ocean, darkening. Who knows
Where the fence runs on the fell?

The fading light, equivocal
As quicksilver, the cloud, the rain
The water singing in its veins,

Leave the earth to dark and wind.

Tweed

I *Source to Peebles*

On the scarred hill, a house with no road.
The burn cuts the brae as an axe pares wood.
The shepherd of Earlshaugh in his tacketty boots
Has set out over the hill without a word.

Dense walls of forest have enfolded him;
Dark crowds of promises. He is swallowed up
With the thieves' road, the Roman road, the iron-age scatterings.
The black trees bleed the valley, drop by drop.

Small mutterings. The restlessness of water. Nothing certain
But its movement and the earth's response. The Powskein; the Corr.
The hills hold the memory of ice and rain. Each hollow
Deepens by the year,

Until there is no house, no road, no miles of forest,
Only the whispering roads of water. Oily, black,
Oozing from mud, glaur, rashers, Tweed begins to murmur:
Never look back.

Peat-red,
Keel-red,
Blood-shot,
Dark at the root,

Down
      it slips,

Last year's pale stalks
Dipping their fingers
In its bitter water.

Squabbling among sedge-spikes,
Horse-tails, the green, primeval

Forest of sponge, spore, spawn,
Peat hag, toad-rush

Bristling among its rusty puddles,
It trickles;
                        twists.

A buzzard brushes the sky with its wingtips.

A hush. A secret.
The first of many meetings.

In the freshest of voices
The oldest of songs

Ripples among Palaeozoic stones,
By boulders, furry as animals,

Among islands of elephantine butterbur,
In deep, slow tributes of golden coins,

Where, like the shadows of the grass, quick as sparks,
Black swarf, flying to the magnet or away from it
In sudden, thrilling rushes, under the water's wrinkled skin,
Salmon parr obey a far-off music.

'I've seen round this table maybe thirty people.
Clippin' started at the valley bottom and y' took your turns.
I loved the meal-times best – the pipe-smoke, the blether.
I sit two weeks now, clippin' on my own.'

Drowsy, creamy meadowsweet,
Crowdie-thick among the bents.
Over the stones, the drones, the chant:

Water's irregular, haunting cadence
Calls them to it, one by one.
Hawkshaw, Menzion, Talla, Fruid –

The little burns sing back to it:

You are the tree and we are the branches.
You are the question and we are the answer.

We are the pages and you are the book.
We are the travellers, you the track.

You are the riddle, and we are the key.
We are the branches, and you the tree.

The hills are accomplices in water.
Secrets. Complicities.
Long feuds.
                    Already
Tweed is assembling its army

By Glenbreck, by Weird Law,
Glenwhappen and Oliver.

Under a roof of ash and sycamore
The dipper curtseys.

The wagtail somersaults,
Light as a gnat.

Between rocky banks,
Green, deep, glassy,
Tweed slides –

Speeds –

And tumbles, torn –
Teems down the linn,
Dives, white spurts
Gushing, leaping,
Drops of spun glass –
Goes over in shreds,
Threads,
A silver loom-warp.

Fresh!

Below, it is milk, frothing in the pail.
It is porridge, seething in the pan.
Fleece, pared away by the clippers.

White strands break from it.
Eddies, crooks,
Whorled like a tup's horn,
Or the ringlets of wool;

Knots in wood. Swirls. Question-marks –
Constellations floating on a milky road.

Then off it slips,
Suddenly hurried –
Tears itself on stones,
Snags, rips itself,
Zigzagging away
To Hartstane, to Polmood,
Flashing its white scuts,
The roar of the linn pursuing it.

And under the echoing arch,
Trapped in the coign,
A white, whirling galaxy
Circles and circles,

Endlessly chasing its tail.

Millstone. Altarstone.
Stone of lost stories:
When does a burn
Become a river?

When does a tale
Forget where it came from?
Hearthstone, whetstone,
Peel and bale-fire.

Stony stillness.
The whisper of water,
The endless turning
Of the sky's grey mill:

Who killed Merlin?
The shepherds of Drumelzier
By the bark-brown water
Under Rachan Hill.

'Forget that,' says Tweed to the grilse,
Climbing her prehistoric road homeward by smell

To the musty, familiar riverbed fug of belonging.
'What's next?' it sings to silurian eels,

Feeling their way down the cool threads of water.
'Tomorrow!' it calls to the sky, to lapwing and plover. The hills

Darken. At Dawyck, at Stobo, rain begins to fall.

Peaceful, worn deep by the long grind,
The steep, solemn valley, filling with pine, oak, ash –
Layer on green layer, rounded as summer cloud-banks –
Cradles the young river in its curves;

And, sinuously, through the ringing leaves –
Blackbird, song-thrush, echoing ever more distant –
Tweed, intent on the future, gathers its forces,

Under the shadowy embrace of seven arches,
Under the iron frown of Neidpath, sprung from the whin,

The blood of two hatreds fused in one green vein.

II *Peebles to Galashiels*

Tittle-tattle Eddlestone, muttering of mill-lades,
Leithen, in harness, chattering of jeannies –
Sluicing down men and women from the hills:

Haad your wheesht, says Tweed
Softly to the Cuddy, the Weaver;
To the dried-up river-beds of labour;
To the stopped mouths of water.

Joe steals down through the Toll Wood in the dark.
He is listening to what the river tells him
Sliding black and silent under the bridge,
Another invisible stream running inside it.

His nets are buried in earth, hung out on branches
Behind the dyke. He knows the hidden places
By touch. He's learnt the river by its voices –
The Red Yett. The Gurley Pool. The Middens.

The pub. The back of a van. A bunch of tenners.
It's a dirty business, fish. Blood, glut, roe, slime.
The Whins. The Strip. The Weaver. Quair Throat.
O, but it's beautiful, the river at night:

Under Lee Penn, beside the whispering
Forest of Traquair, the shivering
Reflections of the flashlight glance and spin.
The salmon sniff the rain upstream. Joe sniffs the salmon.

And using the currents as the salmon use them,
He lets his cairn net curl, caa' back, until,
Drop by gleaming steely drop, the river
Gives up its secrets to him. Then he's off

Over the fence. The dark will swallow him
Like water. *Howden. Cowford. Leithen Pool.*
The Dam. The Cauld. A salmon leaps. Another.
The fish belong to no one but the river.

'Got a romantic idea about poachers?
Don't you believe it. I've been a bailiff
Twenty year, and my father before me.

It's quietened off now. There's not the numbers:
Farmed salmon's finished the market.
I wouldn't go out till night time normally.

When I see a light, that's me on the mobile.
You don't know what they're carrying nowadays.
Slashing your tyres, smashing your vehicle –

Take it from me, they're nought but criminals.'

'I've cleeked them, I've netted them,
I've sneggled and I've guddled them;
I've gumped them in the eel-beds.
We were fin, fur and feather bairns,'

Says Joe.
          'Tweed kept us.

Wi' cairn net, wi' bag net,
Wi' set net an' pullin' net,
It fed us. It claed us.
Put shoon on oor feet.'

And who's to argue?

Not Tweed,
Mingling its strange upwellings,
Its undertows, its cold currents,

Singing over the gravel,
Under the willow,
Over the cauld,

To ragwort-yellow Caberston,
Scrogbank, Rampy Pool,
To Rough Haugh and the Bogle,

You can make laws
Or break laws
But you'll quickly be forgotten:

The fish belong to no one
But the water
And tomorrow.

Stalactites hang
From the arches of Ashiesteil.
At Caddonfoot, at Fairnilee,
At the narrow bridge of Yair,

One by one, the ash trees
Trail their green fingers,
Sending thrills of silver
Through the river's silk,

Shoals of gold that flicker
Over the birch-bark,
Into the quiet forest,
Into the farthest shadows.

Tall reeds. Willows,
A basket, an arrow,
A deer slot, an echo,
Boats of skin and bark:

I was their road.
I kept them. Their shelter,
The forest. Every stalk
Glints, a weapon.

Tiers of trees, their bulk
Broken in the water,
Every fluent shape
Remembered, reconfigured:

Stipple, dapple,
Glitter, ripple,
Chatter, stutter –

To Tweed's next meeting, muster, mingling of vernaculars –
Where Ettrick bowls down from Lindean, jabbering of plague,

From Selkirk, muttering of leather, from Philipshaugh
And Carterhaugh, and the dark forest, garrulous with nightmares,

And gabbles into Tweed

Where thistledown drifts from a disused bridge, and rain
Drips on a triangle of grizzled meadow and, huddled

Still as a heron under their ripped umbrella,
A boy and an old man, bored, not much to go home for,

Watch the current tow their line, while under the trees

Silts, seeds, gravels, spawns, the spring smolt and the autumn,
Twill, twine and herring-bone, and the water jumbles them

To Hart Pool, to Abbotsford, redrafting, dreamily erasing,
Soothing, shepherding them all away, to where

Gala gushes down, muttering of carding sets,
Shuttles, looms, mordents, blue-grey sediments –

All gone, Gala. Hush now, says Tweed.

III *Galashiels to Kelso*

A fisherman reads the river-bed with his feet.
So delicate
The arc of his line as it sings through the air
It is art. It is music. It is all in the timing.

Got my Jock Scott, got my Silver Doctor,
Got my Black Ali Shrimp and my Garry Dog,
Got my Meg with the Muckle Mooth and Hairy Mary,
Got my Logie, my Jeannie, my Temple Dog;

Bring me a black-tipped fillet from a hare's ear,
A harl from a feather in a partridge tail,
A tippet from a pheasant and a gamecock's hackle,
Stoat-hair, squirrel-tuft, red bull poll:
Come, wild spirit –
Catch me a salmon,
Spirit of the earth and sky and hill.

Got my yellow Ali Shrimp, got my Kinmont Willie,
Got my Meg in her Braws and my Dusty Miller,
Got my Cascade Shrimp, got my Stoat and my Comet,
Got my Junction Shrimp. Got my Monroe Killer.

At Elm Well, a heron shakes out its wings,
A grey canvas tent flap. A moorhen scoots to the rushes
And, in the corner of one eye, a kingfisher

Flashes its blue tinsel. And the line sings.
It is art and wildness, dancing together
To the river's music.

It is the deepest magic

In a land of spells, enchantments, whispers
Out of Wedale, out of Lauderdale, stories

Borne down the river like seeds,
Snagged in the heather,
On the whin's thorns;
Asleep under the Eildons.

Three witches. Three naked sisters.
Three sails on a black schooner.
Three teeth on the sky's jawbone:

Three sets of eyes that fix Tweed in one glare.

Towering, gnarled, volcanic, over the valley floor
That heaves, a sea, around them, they hold it spellbound;

And fold on fold, for miles, far fells and moors –
The bare, broad Cheviots, Ettricks, Lammermuirs –

Sullen, wind-torn, disputatious grounds –
Tense with expectation, or with fear.

Cursing the eye that stares into the future,
Winding back time to where it came from,
Three sisters. Three witches.

Three teeth on the sky's jawbone.

Under their shadow, Tweed is slowing, growing older.
Deeper, richer, more abundantly, it blooms,

Green tiers of birch, oak, alder, arching over
Banks of purple loosestrife, balsam and bees,

Reeds, silvery with warblers, and speckled thrushes
Rooting under the sycamores; and never more lovely

Than in the secret woods of Bemersyde,
Rinsed with its thousand birdsongs, dappled with gold,

Around the hushed stones of an older Melrose,
It loops; coils back on itself. Looks over its shoulder.

Prayers in the vaults;
Catechisms in the tracery;
Psalms in the buttresses;

And in the water, arguments.

Conversions. Baptisms. Blessings.
Writhing inside them,
Dark, ancient upwellings.

In an instant, Tweed is an adder.
Red veins dilate in it, anger
Flaring under its leaf-fringe. It is a colt.

As if its hair stood on end,
As if its nerves quickened, its skin trembles;
It breaks into white crests – leaps, churns, tumbles –

It is iron on the anvil,
Spitting cold sparks –
Oystercatchers' shrill shrieks.

It is a lion. The corkscrew torrent
Twists: gnaws
The red shank of rock.

A second later, it stretches, softens; relaxes.
It is a lamb. A shepherd. Its crook
Shelters a flood-plain of buttercups.

Berry Bush. Monksford. Cradle Rock. The Corbies.
Brockies Hole. Kipper Haugh. The Pot. The Webbs. The Bleedies.

It glides under Mertoun bridge, a green lullaby
Singing itself to sleep by Makerstoun,
Dreaming the streams, dubs, pools, the bright miles before it.

The Duke's daughter has caught her first fish!
Isabella has captured a grilse.
It shines, a new moon, trapped in polythene.
Laughing, she runs with it across the lawn

Towards the sunlit turrets. She has brought it
From the smooth surface of the river, where the wind scribbles,
From the cool tunnel of trees, through open meadow
Beside the yellowing mound of Roxburgh Castle.

Great space, great sky surrounds her. Upon so little
So much depends. The river sighs. A fish
Leaps. The widening circles of its ripples
Catch the green sweep of Roxburghshire in a mesh of light.

Behind a door, a desk; a man is writing
Numbers in a ledger. The words 'Income Stream',
Jobs, projections, graphs and calculations
Flicker before him on a computer screen.

He wants to say they are the same: great families, salmon rivers –
Feeding the valley, keeping it green. But Isabella
Bursts from the sunshine through the dark doors, beaming.
She will show her shining burden to her father.

IV *Kelso to Coldstream*

What is making its way downriver,
Bobbing, turning?

A branch. A bucket. A bottle.
Nothing of value.

What is racing through Junction Pool,
Under the bridges,
Past the drowned islands,

Pulling its thread by Milk Pot,
Butterwash, elbowing onwards

Through bean and barley fields,
Through banks of crimson balsam?

It is life:
A bottle. A branch. A bucket.

It is time.
It is nothing of value.

'Every beat's different. Each pool's peculiar.
Half of my work is in conservation.
Fencing, spraying. Keeping it natural.
What do you mean, that's a contradiction?

Hogweed, for instance – if one beat above you
Holds back the spray, it'll be your problem
Next year, look out. The same goes for gravel.
It all carries down to the next stretch of water.

Which is also a lesson in business investment.
The people who fish here – they come from all over;
So anyone making money from salmon
Must pay that money back into the river.

What do I think of traditional netsmen?
They're taking the fish and they give little for them,
No thought for the future. I know it's their living,
But look at it this way – they're just not sportsmen.'

At Birgham a spider has drawn a map of the world,
Itself at the azimuth. All its meridians,

Stretching from clusters of purple campion,
Glint, as the breeze

Sends shivers of light through the ripening barley;
And over the broad, slow water that whispers: *Be still*,

All summer long, a small explosion of swallows
Angles and weaves.

Fifty miles away, the sky is clouding:
Rain darkens Tweedshaws. At Sprouston, the fish taste it.

A thousand miles away, the iron needle
Twitches for Carham in the salmon's icy blood.

Deep in the earth's spool, a spindle is turning.
Slowly, the barley twitches towards autumn.

The eels quiver. The spider thrums. The swallows
Gather the threads of the river, skeins of the world.

The hymn carries down from Flodden
Over the rigs of cut hay,

Over the yellow rape, stubble, the hissing barley
And the bent hawthorn tree;

Over the rich, sweet black and silver midden-heap.
So green,

So still, so drowsy: nothing stirs
Except the wren,

Singing, full-throated,
Fierce, belligerent,

As if it would join in.

What joins us,
               divides us.

Silent,
     relentless,
The valley
        begins
To fill up
        with horses.
The flicker
        of eye-white,
The crimson
        nostril.
From Coldstream,
           from Cornhill,
The Merse
       and Twizell.

And Tweed braids silver
And black, and silver.
The may-fly dances
On the water's skin;

And the valley fills up with the smoking wildness of horses;

The wildness

Of men.

Then Tweed, swift, inaccessible, secret,
Bears the light away through the trees.

The long grass hushes in Lennel churchyard
And the evening breeze

Carries a heather scent from Cheviot.
Warmth and peace

Fall on the lichen-speckled slabs, the roofless chapel open
To the sky,

A rubble of broken headstones for its pavement.
Thistle-scratched, they lie

Scattered, their crusted faces peeling, names erased.
The starlings fly

Up from the ivy-tangled walls: the prayers
That no one heeds.

The dead lie anchored in their little boats among the nettles
And the docken leaves.

Where will the river carry them?
Homeward, says Tweed.

V *Coldstream to Berwick*

Deep, slow, oily, sinister,
Under the viaduct, by the tall poplars,

Hedged by an island of willow and alder,
Gravy-brown soil washes down from the Till,

Darkening Tweed – a stain, a shadow,
An English tune in a similar idiom;
Widdershins swirls of drumly water.

There are two sides to every border.

Shake out your wings, Bob Morrison, Bob Morrison,
The rouk's on the river. When the water-kelpie
Gie's ye a gliff doon at Tillmouth or Twizell,
Haul in your gear, lads – it's time ye were leavin'.

A chill in the afternoon. The vixen
Has signed this path with her scent; the otter
Flattened the grass in its slide to the river

An hour ago. The willow clings to tatters

From last years' floods. Tomorrow's hatchlings
Quicken in the reeds. Inquisitive ducklings
Rootle for caddis-fly. Pondweed shivers.

A lattice of sunlight fractures, glitters.

And, but for the creak of an oar on its thole pin –
The long, slow, indolent strokes of the boatman
Rowing his rod to a sure lie for salmon –

Now is the only moment that matters.

At Great Haugh shiel, the chimney-stack
Sprouts grass. The black felt roof peels back

Like the sole of a boot. A green door creaks
Open. A key rusts in the lock.

High in the rafters' tarry gloom,
Nets rot over a musty room

Where everything's touched with the same soft brush
Of river-mud. It has dried to dust

On the sagging mesh of the five wire berths
In their wooden cupboard, lagged with earth

And camouflaged the walls, the doors,
A shelf of cups and the kitchen chairs

Round the empty hearth. Strewn over the floor,
Crackled, returning to clay, loam, straw,

A rose-patterned plate, a teapot lid.
Though the window is frosted thick with mud,

Sun stipples through it. And over all
A fine, dry silt of silence has fallen,

As if the men had just gathered their coats
From the three tin hooks by the door, and gone;

And after a little while, curious, searching,
The river had come to look for them.

Shake out your wings, Bob Morrison, Bob Morrison –
We've heard the hoolet shoot from Milne Graden
In the broad daylight. We've seen a salmon,
Church key stuck in his thropple like a gob-stick.

Speeding, berrelling under Norham bridge,
Streamers of white froth coil, unroll.

Grabbed fistfuls of black silk surge up, turn over,
Flower and spread, and slowly fold together

In chains, long scrolls,

That peel apart and stream away, their progress
Linking, breaking, spiralling, relentless.

The woods and policies purr with pigeons,
Elegant, civilised. Light as a leaf,
A delicate fly-catcher skims the water,

Meeting its likeness briefly in a mirror,
The banks beyond a blind, primeval forest –
Life, getting on with it. Sudden spokes

Block the light, spike the sun,
Stinking, promiscuous; anything human –
A cauld, a batt, a footing – is annexed.

But what's this?
     Round the next twist,
          under the hogweed,

Just at the bow of the meadow, in sight of the cobweb
Curves of the Union Chain Bridge, under the trees,

Something is trying to claw its way up to the surface
From very deep.

Green swirls.
   Long fingers.
      Weed.
         The musky scent of it.
The salt.

The sea.

'Ye watched the clouds. Ye read the signs –
Ye heard the trains on the Grantshouse line
Long before the north wind blew.
They're aback a the tide an' away t' the river.

A stiff north wind an' the tide holds in
At the Royal Bridge, an' it won't leave Yarrow.
But a west wind an' a big tide
Sucks on the ebb till the banks are dry

An' they'll come on the top a the tide. Ye time it,
Wait for the Point when the tide comes forward –
That's wor harvest, Point. An' mind,
Ye'll never predict a salmon exactly –

That's how they've survived for generations.
Nets have done nothing to damage the river.
Hundreds a' years a' the nettin' stations
An' salmon come back the same as ever.

Now it's off wi' the nets an' it's back to 'nature'.
Whatever wor natural instinct to catch 'em,
A fish on the rod is worth more to the river.
These days it's money keeps things Natural.'

A flash. A gleam. The slap, kick, thump,
Smack on the shore is a shock: five salmon
Out of their element, furious, violent,

Beautiful as a birth. The shining
Muscle and guts of the river loosed
Around their feet, the four men stoop:

A tumult. Wing-beats. For an instant
The same wild current courses through them.

Croak from the reed-beds, Bob Morrison, Bob Morrison,
The rouk's on the water. The border is shiftin' –
From North Bells to Low Bells, it's time we were leavin'.
It's more for the rods and more for the river.

Under the A1's arterial hurry
Old Tweed spreads out, broad and slow and easy,

Its surface feathered by the breeze. All blowsy,
It slops, laps, toothless, at the undercut mud-bank,

A glacial boulder, a traffic cone, a stone-age fish-trap,
Slowly sinking into ooze and slime, or slowly uncovered.

High overhead, their wings up-lit at sunset,
Armies of herring gulls row their white ghosts downriver.

Over the flat haugh, over the salt-marsh, they muster
Out of two countries – over the wheat fields, the ramparts,

The sewage plant, the housing estates, the rotting dockyards,
And drift on Yarrow Slakes like snow – one flock.

At Whitesands and Abstell, Calot and Blakewell,
At Carr Rock, at Crow's Batt, at Gardo an' Hallowstell,
Haul in your gear, lads, it's time we were leavin'
From Canny and Pedwell to Farseas and Sandstell.

Ahead, the Royal Border Bridge. It is a gate
Sorting this side from that side. It combs the broad water.

Beached on the mud-bank, the haughty swans clap their wings:
Here's Berwick, perched on its high horse, looking down on England.

The tide is sucking out. Its swirls and eddies claw away

The knuckled roots of pines and fossil forests, cones and seeds,
The silts, soils, stones of prehistoric oceans dragged from far upstream,

The spawn, the snails, the shrimps, the eels, the smolting salmon – millions strong,
Their populations scattering

To far-flung places of migration and desire, tumbled and whirled
And rolled together in the dark, the cold

Salt, shifting place where river ends and sea begins

To wind all journeys back to where they came from.

It's this that I was looking for,
Says Tweed:

Oblivion.

On Spittal beach, among the sticks and broken shells, strips torn
From desiccated black
Plastic bin-bags metamorphose into crackling scraps
Of bladderwrack,

And tubes of polypropylene become the whumlick kex,
And strands of willow bough,
The hitches, bends and splices of a thousand long-discarded
Nylon tows;

As if, in this great glittering meeting, weaving, marrying, relaxing,
Tweed lets go
Its cumulative weight of contradictions; memories, imaginings – all borders
Flow

Into one another, and the line – the human, managed, measurable shore –
Is lost
To whirling currents; and, beyond, the spiral stream
Of stars and dust.

On the farthest spit of coarse brown grit,
Sandstell,
Wind shivers a few blades of lyme-grass, and the sun picks out
A bleached sheep's skull,

And wound around it, rags and tatters that were once
A salmon net;
So tangled up, their fortunes river-ravelled and impossible
To separate.

3

CASTLE

Shanky

Shanky is all England:
A barn-conversion.
Strangers in four-by-fours. Forgotten

Names: the Butty Meadow. Shanky Hall.
The nugget of a chapel.
Faith in ruins.

Down the Long Nanny Burn
A green gate leans.
Dark, witchy hawthorns

Point along the leat
To Shanky Mill,
Its bricked-up windows, walls

Empty, its rafters open
To the swifts, the rain;
The knotted fabric of the farm

Shrunk, first, to one man
Alone in his tractor cabin,
Radio on; then

To no one
But the nostalgic, who like it here
At nightfall, when

Black cows wallow in the burn
And the low sun
Floods everything golden.

A Short History of Bamburgh

There are many histories: first,
The iron-red castle
Lording over the red-gold sand at sunset.

Next, the sea. How it roars
And quarrels with the islands: Longstone,
Its cold pulse of light.

Then bent-grass and sand. Wind.
Squat willows, bones;
Skylarks' knotwork, twining the whins to Spindlestone;

The Gamestone; the King's Baulk; the Worm Well –
Scraps and make-believe
Forged in the village smithy. What is forgotten

Between the Whistle Wood and the Blue Hemmel
Matters most of all. Tomorrow
There are fields to sow. Deep in the Grove

Rooks, like old priests, squabble.

Dunstanburgh

Loud kittiwakes on an echoey crag:

There is a castle by the sea
That no road leads to any more –

On the height of a cliff, the farthest edge
Of land, a wind-rucked field; a wall

And gatehouse, ruled across the sky;
A city, seen from miles away;

A promise, pledged in tall stone towers
That, more than battle, passing years,

Winter on winter of wind and rain,
Have battered down to a great ruin:

There's a secret as old
As the stones to unlock:
There's a riddle, a mystery
Trapped in the rock,
   In the rock,
   In the rock,
   In the rock,
   In the rock,
   In the rock.

Fade into kittiwakes, merging with them completely.

And nobody visiting listens or stays
Long enough to tell that the noise

Of the sea on the cliff-face does not cease,
Or to say when the swallows and gulls that roost

In its loud, rocky hollows are suddenly gone
To the tug of winter; and nobody sees

How, in its hours of solitude,
The ruin is endlessly reclaimed.

Rift of rock,
Buckle. Twist.
Black scar,
Wrench, ruck.
Cold stone
Crust, crack.

Grey-green lichen,
Brittle, prickly,
Boils and blisters,
Crusty, crackly
Moon-craters,
Pale and warty,
Witches' fingers,
Scabbed and scaly.

Crosswort, stitchwort,
Sea-spurrey, scurvy-grass,
Rest-harrow, meadow-rue,
Shepherd's purse and goose-grass;

Stonecrop, forget-me-not,
Lady's-smock and speedwell;
Mouse-eared chickweed,
Bird's-foot trefoil;

Waregoose, wullymint,
Mullymac an' kittiwake,
Tommy noddy, cuddy duck,
Tudelum an' gormer.

Deed tides, big tides,
Wullymint an' mullymac,
Come, Jack, shine the lowe,
Days is gettin' longer.

The salt wind racks the grass and high
Cirrus; claws the rutted sea –

Rift of rock,
Buckle. Twist.
Black scar,
Wrench, ruck.

Cold stone
Crust,

Crack!

Grey-green lichen,
Brittle, prickly,
Boils and blisters,
Crusty, crackly

Moon-craters,
Pale and warty,
Witches' fingers,
Scabbed and scaly.

Waregoose,
Wullymint,
Mullymac,
Kittiwake,

Tommy noddy,
Cuddy duck,
Tudelum,
Gormer.

Cloud, field, ashlar – each
Surface scored with deep, oblique

Furrows, slant and dissonant;
Music, frozen in perfect silence,

An argument of stone and sky,
Between the things that stream away –

Tear, race, fly – and those that stand;
Between the marks of human hands

And marks of frost and tide and wind.

Scratched and slanted,
Flurried, ruffled,
Whipped, wealed,
Ridged and rippled,
Grooved, scarred,
Meshed, barred,
Acid-pitted,
Pocked and stippled:

Go sky,
Wind-blown
Cloud, sea.
Stay, stone.

Oven-red,   Scratched
Sulphur-yellow,   And slanted,
Thunder-dark,   Flurried, ruffled,
Flesh-sallow,   Whipped, wealed,

Wind-clawed,   Ridged and rippled,
Storm-driven,   Grooved,
Field-furrowed,   Scarred,
Cloud-riven,   Meshed,

Pigeon-grey,   Barred,
Sky-blown,   Acid-pitted,
Sea-swept   Pocked
Sandstone.   And stippled:

Go sky,
Wind-blown
Cloud, sea.
Stay, stone.

Stay, stone.
Fly, go,
Sea, sky,
Wind-blown.

Inside tower:

All day, all night, the wind explores
The gaps, the cracks. The stones resist.

As if it was searching for something lost,
The wind interrogates the walls.

Through arrow-slit, down parapet,
Round inaccessible, remote

Corners – a peaceful window-seat,
Marooned like something beyond the tide –

The wind inquires. Round battlements,
Up spiral stairs, through chambers, halls,

Brimful of voices, the way a shell
Fills with remembered sounds of the sea,

It pries. It probes.
The castle echoes:

It has become the wind's instrument.

Outside. Kittiwakes:

It's an island of rock.
It's a dragon, asleep,
With a dinosaur back
And the tail of a beast.
    It's a beast,
    It's a beast,
    It's a beast,
    It's a beast,
    It's a beast.

Fade out kittiwakes.

Hanging Stones:
Who?
      A dozen
Basalt towers,
Faceless, frozen;
Iron-armoured,
Rust-red,
Hacked, cracked,
Cold blood

Automata, black and blind,
Prehistory, glowering out,
They hold the tower aloft,
Offering it to the sky,
Lifting it up, cold hands
Raised in sacrifice
To sun and star and wind.

Wind that brings iron and timber,
Takes sons, brings strangers,
Wind that fans the fire's hunger –
    Whisper. Whisper. Who lives here?

What did he have on his mind,
The architect who planned
The hilt of a sword, stuck
In the spine of the rock –
What was he thinking of?

We know, hiss the stones.

Sudden skylark.

Build me a tower. Make it high,
Like a city set on top
Of a hill, let it be seen
Like a landmark for a ship,
Like a dagger in a fist,
Or like a claw, or like a crest,
Or like a warrior, one sprung
From the seed of standing stones,
Or like an angle-iron, strong,
Or like a snarl, a scowl, a frown,

74

Or like a riddle in the rock,
Or like a key without a lock,
Or like a head upon a block,
Or like a crown upon a king.

Find me a spring. Dig me a lake
To surround my tower. Make
A silver island of the mind.
Let it shiver in the wind,
That, like a meeting with a twin,
Or like a ghost beneath a glass,
Or like a mirror and a face,
Or like an echo from the past,
Like a lily, like a swan,
Like a vision or a dream,
You may read it as a sign,
The reflection of the stone
Like the pages of a book,
Like a sword fast in a rock,
Or like a key without a lock,
Or like the Isle of Avalon.

Sea. Kittiwakes, loud:

In the city of kittiwakes everyone's scolding
The comings and goings,
The restless arrivals,
Departures, the shuffling
To-ings and fro-ings;

With their clean yellow beaks,
Their iron-grey backs,
Salt-white breasts
And their wings dipped in darkness.

White wings of a kittiwake
Sheer off the cliff
In a deep sickle dive
Into empty air
To soar, and circle.

And back comes the babble –
Peremptory cries

That rise to a higher, angrier echo –
Angular splashes against the slow
Undertone of the sea.

And he's back again,
To elaborate greetings:
Head-shaking,
Billing,
Fencing twin beaks,
Excitedly weaving two heads back and forward
While everyone shrieks,
And the entire city
Grinds into gear to announce the arrival.

A snowstorm of kittiwakes, shaken, won't settle,
In the shanty-town,
In the high-rise huddle,
The tenement squalor,
The squabble and babble.

There's a secret as old
As the stones to unlock:
There are bones in the soil –
Something sleeps in the rock.
    In the rock,
    In the rock,
    In the rock,
    In the rock,
    In the rock.

Kittiwakes swallow up this end, then fade out.

Hauled out like boats, the eider ducks
Warble and preen on the barnacled rocks.
There are sparkles sewn on the folds of the sea.

Far below, a metallic clatter:
A cormorant struggles out of the water,

Ungainly till airborne. Landlocked, another
Folds up his wings like an old, black umbrella.

On the scurvy-grass cliff-top, ice-white,
A fulmar peels, the blade of a knife,
From the rind of the black rock into the light;

And where the sea-pinks rustle their dresses,
Where the salt wind combs the grass,
A tatty sea, its shadow crosses

Over the edge, and by its straight
And soundless flight, the land is blessed.

Waregoose, wullymint,
Mullymac an' kittiwake,
Tommy noddy, cuddy duck,
Tudelum an' gormer.

Deed tides, big tides,
Wullymint an' mullymac,
Come, Jack, shine the lowe,
Days is gettin' longer.

Sea on rocks, echoey:

Bare Gull Crag sees little sun.
Wrinkled whinstone, ancient skin,

Scabbed and ring-wormed, brutal, alien,
Hunches down beneath the wind.

Cold rock. Musty blocks
Softened by the nap of a velvet moss,

Stained with streaks of rust and purple,
Iron-rich; burned autumnal

Fiery gold and moon-white crystal,
Compost-green and crimson mineral,

Feed the lichens' grey-green spores
On the prehistoric shore.

There's a secret as old
As the stones to unlock:
There are bones in the soil –
There's a child in the rock.
   It's a child,
   It's a child,
   It's a child,
   It's a child,
   It's a child.

Wind that brings iron and timber,
Takes sons, brings strangers,
Wind that fans the fire's hunger –
Whisper. Whisper. Who lives here?

There's a longing, a promise,
The key to a spell:
There's a terrible choice
We are fated to fail.
   There's a choice,
   There's a choice,
   There's a choice,
   There's a choice,
   There's a choice.

Gentle sea hushing:

Good lordship, she's a quiet sea,
Slack tide an' a fair breeze
And nets a harrin'.

Bad lordship is a gale a wund,
The boat adrift or owertorned
And wrecken.

Hush, hush of sea.

Good lordship brings the shoowers an' sun
Tae swell the ear o' the corn
In hor right season.

Bad lordship is the nest awa',
The eggs smashed, the corbie craa'
Amang the clecken.

Hush of sea.

78

At the height of June it is barely night
For the blink of an eye. In the two a.m. twilight

The fields stir and wake.
                    Disembodied larks
Sing to each other in the dark,
Over the bent-grass, under the stars;

First one, then many; invisible webs
Enmeshing the dunes like spider-threads
Embroidering the cool black air –

Messengers from another shore,
Close, and unreachable. Before

Dark solidifies into day,
The whole land holds its breath and waits,
Belonging neither to night nor morning.

Whir of wings.

Up on the height of its glorious hill,
The five-storey, silent, empty

Shell of the gatehouse floods and brims
With noise, gold, firelight, dancing;

And like an old heart that is tired of living,
That suddenly kindles with something like joy,

The hollow walls are brimful of music.
The minstrels have come to the gallery.

Swallows singing inside gatehouse:

And the swallows are needles,
Blue-black arrows,

Ravelling breathtaking streamers of flight,
Making doors out of windows,
Effortless shadows,
Wreathing the castle in flickering light

Between silence and sunrise,
Darkness and daybreak,
Emptiness and music,

Between ecstasy and heartbreak.

Fade out swallows. Outside, distant kittiwakes:

There's a secret as deep
As the sea. In the dark
At the heart of the rock
There's a fault. There's a crack.
   There's a child,
   There's a child,
   There's a child,
   There's a child,
   There's a child.

Fade out kittiwakes.

An August night. Above the clouds
Over the Egyncleugh, the moon

Rises. The wind is slowing down,
The world relaxing into sleep.

Not a bird on the water. Only the hush
Of the long grass, and the sea's wash,

And the slightest stir of birds on the cliff –
A cleared throat, a chuckle, a cough:

A ship of sleepers cast adrift.
A crane-fly whirs. Papery moths,

Water-marked wings the colour of stone,
Drift through the thistles; and the moon,

Climbing, draws a path across
The darkening water; phosphorus

Catching the ripples as they run
In liquid silver, a seething shoal
Of scales and fire.

                    The castle walls
Loom higher in the dark, a great
Wrecked ship. The moon illuminates

Its cargo – feathery grasses, lichens,
Spokes of hogweed, may-crown plantains,

Daisies, studding the decks like stars.
Its brightness calls, and all light things answer.

In the courtyard, around the foundations,
The kitchens, the chapel, the Constable's chambers,

Leathery wings flit. Woodlice trundle,
Armour on stone. A spider trembles,

A web's bulls-eye in the moon's full glare.
On the arc of its journey, fierce white fire

Catches and fills a heart-shaped window.

And the deepest dark of the castle walls –
Doors going nowhere, hearths, holes,

Garderobes, stairways bent at odd angles –
Join with the wider dark, the miles

Of field and heugh, and wind-blown fell,

Millennia of dark, the men
And women lost beyond recall,

Absorbed in silence, earth and stone.

Oot a the neet
Wi'oot a soond,
Ower the heather
An' benty groond,
Ower the moors

An' ower the mosses,
Th' grab wor kye,
Th' steal wor hosses,
Th' raid wor hemmels
An' byres an' steeds
An' born wor hooses
Aboot wor heeds.

Th' come like the wund
Or the snaa' in June.
Th'll gollup the meat
For' off yee'r spoon.
Th'll tyek yee'r spindle,
Yee'r kist an' quern,
An' strip the blanket
For' off the bairn;
They'll whup the sark
For' off'n yee'r back,
Then trapple yee'r barley
An' fire yee'r stacks.

Th' bring nae baggage
An' when they've fled
Leave nowt but widders
An' empty beds;
Empty bellies
An' hairts as sair
As fields a stubble
And esh. Aah sweer,
Though this be the country
God forgot,
The divvil receive
The reivin' Scot!

Eerie bird noises – curlew, oystercatchers.

The stones smell smoky. Bracken rusts
On the bank. Pools of mist

Make an island of the hill
Around the heugh. Along the wall,

Creeping deep, wet, soot-black stains
Mottle the ashlar, streaked like flames.
Nettles blacken in the rain.

In garderobe, chimney, damp green gloom
Of low, cold-ceilinged sentry-rooms,

In fusty corners, upside down,
Shut butterflies have turned to stone.

Under the water-trough squats a toad.
Its squashy sides squeezing like bellows,

It stretches, blinks.

                From somewhere high,
Far and lifted up, a cry

Prickles the skin and stirs to flight –
A fear, a fire in the night,
A spark in tinder – catches light,

Till every living thing stiffens and stops
To listen.
          Geese!
              The chain unclasps

And fastens again in the watery sky.

Oxen, they brought, and sheep,
And the things they carried,

All they possessed on earth –
A blanket, a net, an axe –

Their cobles, crops, homes
Burned, and the wind harried

The smoke across the fields
From Little Mill to Brunton.

We herded them like sheep.
They slept in sheds, with oxen.

Then one night in the dark
We heard them softly singing:

'The stories that we carry
Will not be burned or stolen;

The castle is an ark
That carries us to safety.'

The stories that we carry
Will not be burned or stolen;

The castle is an ark
That carries us to safety.

Loud gust of wind. Inside tower:

There's a feud that is spread
On the wind by a word,
Like a spark in a stackyard,
A plague in the blood.
There's one law for some.
It's the way things are done.
Is it justice you seek?
It's a son for a son.

It gnaws at the heart
As a dog chews a skull,
Down the ladder of years
As the wind gnaws the sills;
As the sea grinds the shore
It deepens, grows old.
It's a refuge we seek
From the wind and the cold.

It's a statement of strength;
It's a threat; and to all
Who are blown with the thistledown
Over the fell,
It's an ark in a storm,
It's a shelter from harm,
It's a harbour, a haven,
A welcome home.

It's a home,
It's a home,
It's a home,
It's a home,
It's a home.

A knife hilt. A belt tag. A stirrup. An ink well.
A penny. A pitcher. The bit from a bridle.
A tin spoon. A flagon. A bone comb. A bangle.
A glass bead. A button. A hinge and a spindle.

Th' bring nae baggage   *Oot a the neet*   *There's a feud that is spread*
An' when they've fled   *Wi'oot a soond*   *On the wind by a word,*
Leave nowt but widders   *Ower the heather*   *Like a spark in a stackyard,*
An' empty beds;   *An' benty groond,*   *A plague in the blood.*
Empty bellies   *Ower the moors*   *There's one law for some.*
An' hairts as sair   *An' ower the mosses,* *It's the way things are done.*
As fields a stubble   *Th' grab wor kye,*   *Is it justice you seek?*
And esh. Aah sweer,   *Th' steal wor hosses,* *It's a son for a son.*
Though this be the country *Th' raid wor hemmels* *There's one law for some.*
God forgot,   *An' byres an' steeds,* *It's the way things are done.*
The divvil receive   *An' born wor hooses* *Is it justice you seek?*
The reivin' Scot!   *Aboot wor heeds.*   *It's a son for a son.*

Wind that brings iron and timber,
Takes sons, brings strangers,
Wind that fans the fire's hunger –
Whisper. Whisper. Who lives here?

Advent. A visit. The hall,
The high table; the Earl
And starry retinue –
A hundred of them, or more,

Seated at table below.
Laughter, noise. The glow
And heat of a crackling fire
Roasting their cheeks; their shadows

Dancing on the wall
Weave and twine. The smell
Of gravy: rabbit, veal,
Steaming roast mutton and ale;

The rustling folds of their clothes,
Plum-coloured velvet and gold
Brocade, and bear-fur; the wool
Tapestries on the wall

Vivid with leaves and flowers,
Wreathes of ivy and rose.
On the rush-scattered floor, as still
As funerary stone,

The hunting dogs doze and dream
Of hot, salt blood on the tongue.
And listen: high overhead,
Rising above the hum

And clatter of voices –
High as the clouds of heaven
Over the Earl, the sun
Piercing the shadows – music:

Trumpet, pipe, drum.

And into the hall, in a flash, flies a sparrow –
Out of the dark of the western window,

Cold on its wings, its small heart racing,
Over the hundred heads, unnoticed,

Never pausing, not for a moment,
Not for an instant's rest or stillness –

Darts, unswerving, true as an arrow
Out of the hall through the eastern window

Into the all-embracing darkness.

Sea that gives salt and herring,
Sea that bears the sun each morning,
Sea that swallows all its children –
    Whisper. Whisper. Who lives here?

Outside. Wind and sea, loud:

86

It is snowing. First, a rattle –
Ice splinters; rose petals.

White fields, black scars:
Far fells disappear;

Heugh and hilltop hunker down.
Whin tangle, hawthorn;

Then the face of walls, the stone
Bleached with snow-flowers, feather-blown.

Beside the grange, a scarlet streak –
An oystercatcher's blood-red beak

The only coloured thing in sight,
As on the tops of walls, snow settles,

On the green between the bristles
Of the moss. The sea is metal,

Boiling, thunderous. The white
Gulls, whipped up, are flecks of ice,

Shattered from the breakers. Foam,
Sea-flung, fizzes on the snow.

Sudden burst of storm noise – very loud:

Sea, milk-white in the Egyncleugh:
Shape-shifter, twister. Two sides
Boil, *(Boom!)* a confluence
That cracks like cannon-fire,
Spits up, *(Crash!)* volcanic,
Smashes in beads of glass –

And there is a frozen moment of stillness –
Before it folds *(Ssssss)*, falls back
Into itself, white silk, hissing,
Just as the next surge rushes, pressing
Forward, swells and plunges, crashing
(Ssssssssshhhhhhhhhh)
Over the black.

On King Henry's shore, a heap
Of filthy rags and bone – a sheep,

A shipwreck, trailing spars and rigging,
Beards of fleece and skin. The straggling

Seaweed streamers of its guts –
Rubber bands, ravelled mats –

Hang from its rafters, ribs and spine;
And round its forelegs tangle twine,

Fishing nets and bladderwrack.
It has begun the long road back

To element and mineral.

Its socket glares. A blue–black fly
Sizzles in its empty eye,

And in the clean, salt, cold sea wind
Among the stones, its jawbone grins.

Queen Margaret has come from France.
The wind blows, and the grass
Trembles before it. Ice
Cracks on the pools like glass.

Over Queen Margaret's Tower
Five white swans,
Straight and clean as arrows,
Head for the south. My friend,

Who can we trust? Whose word
Is neither ice nor grass
Nor the shifting wind?
Over the field in-bye,

Shadow under its wings,
Hunger in its belly,
A chestnut kestrel bends,
Its eye stitched to its prey.

Quiet sea:

The immense quiet of evening: things
Returning home.
Stone that was bone in the morning and gold at three
Is only stone.

Now the flat, slate sky is feathered
Like a pigeon's breast,
Lilac, fiery pink and smoky grey
And, in the west,

Over Alnwick Moor and Hedgeley, flags
Of crimson flame
Blaze up from Cheviot, turning
Rock-pools to bloodstains.

It's a job for a friend,
It's a word in your ear,
It's a favour returned,
It's a sweetener, my dear;
It's the way things are done
With a gift or a name,
It's a well-oiled machine:
It's the patronage game.
>   *It's a game,*
>   *It's a game,*
>   *It's a game,*
>   *It's a game,*
>   *It's a game.*

It's the strong and the weak.
It's a favour, I fear;
And, behind a locked door,
It's a word in your ear.
It's the way things are done.
It's a safe house for some.

It's a job for a friend,
It's a word in your ear,
It's a favour returned,
It's a sweetener, my dear;
It's the strong and the weak.
It's a favour, I fear;

89

It's the way power speaks
From the mouth of a gun.
It's a bolt in your back
Or a knife to your neck.
Is it justice you seek?
You'll be lucky, my friend.

And, behind a locked door,
It's a word in your ear.
It's the way things are done
With a gift or a name,
It's a well-oiled machine:
It's the patronage game.

Now the land grows dark.
Yellow lichen glows,
Fluoresces on the tops.
The square foundations hold
The silver of the sky
In gritty puddles, while
The colours slowly drown,
Drain away, and stone
Sedimentary clouds
Ease up out of the west;
The walls, the fiery grass,
One coal, slowly cooling.

Then Longstone, miles away,
Sweeps its glassy beam
Over the slant sea's
Rig and furrow. Home
It calls the unnumbered gulls
Oaring over the waves,
Threading between the shadows,
Winding their long wake home.
Round it wheels – the days',
The years' pulse – summoning
The last light left on earth,
The silver of the sea.

Wind that brings
Iron and timber,
Takes sons,
Brings strangers,
Wind that fans
The fire's hunger –
Whisper. Whisper.
Who lives here?

Whisper. Whisper.
Who lives here?

Quiet, inside tower; whistling wind:

My job's to watch. I guard this gate.
All night I hear the sea's low roar
Deep in the Egyncleugh, the sore
Wind around the battlements.
This is a melancholy place.
Through every loophole, gaping pit
And arrow-slit, the cold wind blows,

90

And all we want from life is peace.
It's peace, Lord.

Sometimes, when the fires are lit,
And we are bored with ale and dice,
And tired of squabbling and fights,
I doze, and dream:
                              A winter's night.
Hooves on the hill. Slant wind and sleet.
Who is it hammers at the door?
I draw the bolts. You fall inside,
Exhausted, aching just to sleep.
But no; not yet. For down a stair
Cut in the rock I lead you.
                                        Now
Imagine the thing you most desire –
The deepest longing in you – lies
There, in the dark, just out of reach,
Calling you. You have a choice –
To shout for help, or face your fate,
Your future, and prepare to fight;
And every fibre of you knows,
To meet that longing, you must choose
Right. But you are tired, so tired...
The dark spins round...In every life
This moment comes.
                              And then I dream
I call three witnesses to speak:

Call the maker, the creator
Of the castle walls, the father
Of the lakes, the gates and harbour;
Call all his strength, his power: to match
His castle's high estate, to watch
And guard and govern – judge, deliver
Virtue here on earth, and measure
Truth against its glassy mirror.

Next, call the snowflake spinner, sweeper
Over the sea, the shifter, shaper,
Stealer of sons, the twister, breaker,
Stone-scratcher, cloud-chaser –
Call the wind – destroyer, seeker.

What do you seek?
               I dreamed a city
Rose from a hill above the sea –
A hope, a pledge, a memory
Of hope, a ghost beneath a glass,
A shining prophecy of peace.
Its lakes, its slender towers – a high,
Right aim, a journey's end, a thing
So beautiful, you stop, and gasp, and stare.

I call the King.

               There is no answer.
Nothing. No one there.

                    There is war, there is peace.
                    In the intimate place
                    At the heart of the rock
                    There's a fault. There's a crack.
                         There's a child,
                         There's a child,
                         There's a child,
                         There's a child,
                         There's a child.

I'm tired of dreams. What do I care
For dusty old romances here,
With little to eat and nothing to do   *There's a sword in the rock.*
But warm myself at the fire and wait   *There's a splinter of glass*
For news that never comes? God knows,   *In the heart. In the soul*
This is a melancholy place.   *There's a terrible choice –*
                                                  Is it peace?
                                                  Is it peace?
                                                  Is it peace?
                                                  Is it peace?
                                                  Is it peace?

All night I watch this gate. I sit
And listen to the sea, the roaring
Wind, and think, when you are called
To choose, to speak, will you choose right?

And what I ask of you is this –
The king we killed – between that shining
City and these roofless walls,
Between that promise and the sword –
Tell me, which of them was his?
He could not give us what we need,
Though all we need on earth is peace.

It's peace, Lord.

Quiet.

Outside, dripping water syncopated with the stresses of the words:

From the bony stones of the rough sea-wall,
Regular as heartbeats, drips fall.

Drips gather, fatten, spill
Down the stairs of the stones, from inky wells

And glistening pools: in stuccoed rooms
And caves of lichen, flowers bloom;

In ferny forests, waterfalls;
And chandeliers in glittering halls;

And their almost inaudible, silvery sound
As the cracked stone thaws and the drops drip down,

Down, is the sound of a spell undone,
Rousing, waking frozen stone.

Fade up kittiwakes, far off:

There's a sword in the rock.
There's a splinter of glass
In the heart. In the soul
There's a terrible choice –
    Is it peace?
    Is it peace?
    Is it peace?
    Is it peace?
    Is it peace?

At the heart of the rock
There's a fault. There's a crack.
In the heart, in the soul
There's a splinter of glass.
    There's a choice,
    There's a choice,
    There's a choice,
    There's a choice,
    There's a choice.

End kittiwakes.

From a hole in the seaward wall, a snail
Stretches its foreparts, eases its tail,

Oozing over the knobbly grain,
Smoothing the stone with its slimy trail.

Its skirts slacken under it. Stretching one eye
To examine a patch of leafy lichen,

It feels its way down a ribbon of silver,
Studded with seashells, ancient mortar,

Fossil of top-shell, cowrie, lime
Sliding under it. Taking its time.

Its slow mouth working, its gluey strings
Trembling in the breeze like skin,

It slithers over root and stalk
And crevice, the sepulchral dark

Hollow of the sea wall, where
The empty shell's reoccupied –

Invisible creatures twitch inside
An alabaster palace, made

In a single movement, from the twist
Of its newel post to its silky lip,

And everything circular starts again.

Kittiwakes, with sea — active, noisy:

Waregoose, wullymint,
Mullymac an' kittiwake,
Tommy noddy, cuddy duck,
Tudelum an' gormer.

Deed tides, big tides,
Wullymint an' mullymac,
Come, Jack, shine the lowe,
Days is gettin' longer.

And the sky is stone:
A rook glides over
Stratified distances,
Deposits of silver;

Heugh, cliff,
Egyncleugh,
The land's slow slide
To the edge of water.

The sky is streaming,
The silvered grass
Running away,
The light, racing:

Go sky,
Wind-blown
Cloud, sea.
Stay, stone.

Oven-red,
Sulphur-yellow,
Thunder-dark,
Flesh-sallow,

Wind-clawed,
Storm-driven,
Field-furrowed,
Cloud-riven,

Go, sky!

Stay, stone!

Pigeon-grey,
Sky-blown,

95

Sea-swept
Sandstone.

Skull-stone	*Oven-red*
Snake-stone	*Sulphur-yellow*
Face-stone	*Thunder-dark*
Fist-stone;	*Flesh-sallow,*
Barred and	*Wind-clawed*
Brindled	*Storm-driven*
Tiger-	*Field-furrowed*
Stripe-stone;	*Cloud-riven,*
Redwood	*Pigeon-grey*
Stained stone	*Sky-blown*
Water-marked	*Sea-swept*
Grain stone;	*Sandstone:*
Biscuit and	*Go, sky —*
Bread-stone;	
River-bottom	*Stay, stone.*
Mud-stone;	
Ocean	*Oven-red*
Mountain	*Sulphur-yellow*
Map-of-the	*Thunder-dark*
World-stone;	*Flesh-sallow,*
Eye-socket	*Wind-clawed*
Knuckle-bone	*Storm-driven*
Field-furrow	*Field-furrowed*
Blown-stone;	*Cloud-riven,*
Red-gold	*Pigeon-grey*
Honeycomb	*Sky-blown*
Bone-marrow	*Sea-swept*
Blood-stone.	*Sandstone.*

Sea that gives salt and herring,
Sea that bears the sun each morning,
Sea that swallows all its children —
    Whisper. Whisper. Who are we?

> *The stories that we carry*
> *Will not be lost or stolen.*
> *The castle is an ark*
> *That carries us to safety.*

> Kittiwakes — fade out.

4

SEA ROADS

The Sea Road

I *Howick*

The land is bent-grass and forest,
One dark mystery.
We turn our faces to the sea, a door.

The moon draws a path on the water.

Road of the silky herring,
Cold slivers of moonlight; road of the sollan,
Threading its white necklaces between the waves;

Road of the wanderers: swallow, stealing
Warmth from the sun on its long streamers;
Snow-bunting, bringing a gift of bare branches;

We bury our dead among the bents,
The sea, a road for them to travel –

Sun-wheel road. Road of tilt and arch –

Fulmar, seal, whale.

II *Lindisfarne*

The sea is a slant road, its scarp
Bears dreams away; sons.

Brings sails, voices, fire
That pricks the back of the neck with fear.

Road of grunts, howls,
Hammer blows; prows
Shearing the sea's furrow,

Each eye an axe; each ship
A nest of wasps.
Wolves. Cold, starved

Road of the word of God.

Salt road: tears, blood.

III *Boulmer*

If there is a road to the sunrise,
A road the stories travel down,

This is it: Addi's road. Isaac's.
A path of silver, red wine,

Black powder, skinned dogs,
Desire, pure as gin.

IV *Alnmouth*

Turnstone and oystercatcher pin
The tide's hem, not an end
Of land, but the road's beginning.

Road of wheat that flows down the turnpike,
Road of Best Peruvian Guano;
Road of heatstroke,

Frostbite, heartbreak; Archangel, Odessa,
Burma; white sails; the world
Opening like an oyster

As it always has, to the swallow, to the white tern
That skims the ocean tilt in search
Of continuous daylight,

And to the salmon, each one
A cold path of moonlight, its brain
A spelk of iron, exact as a pin.

Stinky

When you draw up here,
Down the hill to the rocket house,
The whitewashed Square

Brined in the past, that redolence
Of tarred rope, oak bark,
Rum casks,

And you lie awake
In the early dawn to catch the sun
Crawl up between

Billy, the coastguard watch-house,
And the castle;
While a robin

Scries from the pan-tiles
Of the hemmel,
And not one coble

Carves its wake
Through the flawless blue silk
Of the Haven,

You might be forgiven
For forgetting
This: the place

Was pigs, middens, yeddle,
Rotten kelp,
Fish livers reeking in the yetlin;

That the roof above your head
Is a tree, its roots
In herring guts.

'Stinky' was the local name for Low Newton-by-the-Sea. The Square is now in the care of the National Trust. 'Billy' is the fishermen's name for the coastguard watch-house at Low Newton, *c.* 1829.

Lovely Day

Vanishing,
         Bobbing up,
                  Vanishing,
                           North of the Buoy,
The *Supreme* dips and disappears in Beadnell Bay,

Dark speck among mountainous seas of molten silver.

'Ye've missed your chance, now, Eddie. Lie where y' are.'

John's on the pier, on the wireless, winding him in.

'Now! Put some speed on!' She surges ahead. From behind,
A huge, bruise-coloured roller – *'Whoa! Eddie!'* – catches her stern

And heaves her –
                Yawing,
                        See-sawing –
                                Towards the sun.

Down she slides, backwards, afloat still; while the sea roars on.

'Now, gan! Haa'd north a bit. Norrard.' Eddie turns her
Head to the pier, as the next surge carries her, riding –

Up, forward,
                Momentarily surfing –
                            Subsiding.

And suddenly she is through it, into flat water
And a pool of sun; and milky behind her
The shaken sea, the shock of the breaking waves.

On the pier, a woman walking her terrier, smiles:

'Hello John –
                Lovely day!'

Coble Counting Song

Eight boats moored in Beadlin Hyeven.
Woman looks oot an' she sees just seven.

A stoene for the drooned in Beadlin chorchyard:
Sometimes a woman can see ower-much, lad.

A poond a foot, a poond a foot,
A poond a foot a cowble cost.

BK 6 was a Boulmer cowble,
Changed hor name for' the *Mary Twizell*:

Fowerteen drooned in a blinnd snaa' flurry.
Hoo much grief can a cowble carry?

A poond a foot, a poond a foot.

Five was the cowbles sailed for' Beadlin
Roond t' the Clyde t' fish for harrin';

Forth an' Clyde was the gates a heaven,
Hell was the timm'ers an' a sail t' sleep in.

A poond a foot, a poond a foot.

Fower was the last crew ontae Longstone
Night a the Blizzard i' the line-time. Someone

Spied 'em driftin' ower the Kni'stone;
That much ice that he scarcely knew them.

A poond a foot, a poond a foot.

Three was the crew a the boat *Provider* –
Sank an' drooned steamin' hyem t' Craster;

Ran away on a sooth-east lipper,
Broadside ontae the sea, booled ower.

Cowble's a grand boat heed t' weather;
Runnin' afore it – divvin't bother.

A poond a foot, a poond a foot.

Tew was the sea-byeuts yen man's widder
Hid in a cupboard wi' the hard, black sorrer

Shut at the bottom of hor throat forivvor.
Tew is a number bad t' shatter.

A poond a foot, a poond a foot.

Yen was a skipper from the Heedlan' Fish Quay,
May God rest him and bless his family.

A cowble was nivvor a boat for yen.
Yen is a number that ends in naen.

Tell me what, noo tell me what,
Aye, tell me what a cowble cost.

All the incidents referred to in this poem are true. A memorial stone in Beadnell churchyard records the loss of four members of the Fawcus family, drowned within sight of home, on 31 January 1885. The *Mary Twizell* was one of four cobles lost from Blyth and Newbiggin with fourteen lives in a snowstorm on 18 March 1915. The Blizzard referred to in stanza seven took place on 6 February 1895: a Seahouses coble was lost with two lives and many Seahouses and Beadnell fishermen took shelter on the Farne Islands. The *Provider* was lost from Craster on 10 February 1928 with three lives. Hartlepool fisherman Edward Bissell was lost from his coble *Bonny Lass* on 18 January 2006. 'A poond a foot' was said to be what it cost to build a coble in the late 19th century.

The Wund an' the Wetter

When God med the world it was wetter an' wund,
An' he stairted in Beadlin, wheer maist things begin.
Folks them daes had nowt but theer words an' theer work
An' some couldna read, but bi God, th' could taalk.
I' the fishermen's hyems, wi' the bairns at their feet
An' the mushels t' skeyn an' the hyeuks aa' t' bait,
Bi the lowe a the fire they'd crack on aa' neet.
An' laugh? Ye wad dee! Ye might no could mek oot
Through the tarry stife aa' th' blethored on.
But the young'uns was saa'ted like harrin' in yon.

Noo it's hard, when ye see folks bowed-ower an' crined,
Tae imagine back sae mony yeers tiv a time
When th're rash as a leveret, fit as a flee
An' kittle as whuppets t' stairt the sea.
Did th' finnd skyul rough? Sorra, haa'd yeer tongue!
The maister mony a time ga' them wrang;
They'd git a fair yarkin' for yammerin' on,
Or a skelp a the lug. For the words that th' used
Wore no reight – th' wore thick a bit; coarse an' gey cruse
Wi' the soonds on a life that was hootchin' fu'
Wi' divvilment, gliffs an' vexations. Nae skyul
Could a haaden that. Then, at the lowsin', a row
Like gollupin' guffies, a blarin' a yowes;
Aa' squaa'kin' an' squealin' – the soond a theer words
Like a poke fu' a starkies an' sicenlike bords:

Gormers an' sollans,
Tarrees an' tudelems;
Sea-mice, waregeese,
Scoots an' teerums,
Pees'its, pilots, little pickies,
Cuddy ducks an' tommy noddies,
Wittery-wagtails, wullymints
An' mullymacs, that cockle an' spit.

An' it's nae bother at aa';
Aa' the tier ye dae
Is clash 'em oot. Forgit the nyems –
We'll nivvor be wantin' them things ageyn:

Hoy the rubbish away –
The bairns' blethor, the fishermen's clatter,
Come wi' the wund an' gan wi' the wetter...

The tuck, the butt, the byennie, the bratt,
The blackjack, the podler, the muckle sea-cat,
The piker, the skeldy, the finner, the plasher,
The paddle-hoosh an' the fatther-lasher,
An' beasties wi' nyems tha' ye'd nivvor believe
Tha' craa' through the wares an' git fast i' the creeves:

Pipers, wi' lang legs like frogs,
Orchins, wi' a thoosand progs,
Soockers an' boockies,
Doggers an' pillin's,
Tyed-legs, kyel-frones,
Musk-shells, pap-stoenes,
Pistils an' nancies an' sixpenny-men...

But we'll nivvor be wantin' them things ageyn
For it's nae slavver at aa'
T' hoy the rubbish away –
Ower she gans, the frones an' the swatters,
Come wi' the wund an' gan wi' the wetter,
We'll noe be wantin' 'em noo...

Aah can mind the time when the men wad stand
On the top a the bank lookin' oot for' the land,
An' the soond a theer crack was as good as a sang
As th' reeled off the marks th' had lorned for sae lang:
For' Langoth an' Collith t' Comely Carr,
For' the Bus a' the Born t' the Shad an' the Bar,
Faggot, the Styenny Hyels, Fiddler's Fyace,
The Cock Craa' Stoene an' thon hob-hard place
At Herrod's Hoose Plantin on Aa'd Weir's hut;
The Chorch on the Black Rock, wheer ye shoot
Sooth for' the smooth at the Benty Gut:
T' the Cundy Rock an' the trink i' the sand
Reight ablow Featherblaa' – by, she was grand.
Ye could listen aa' neet. Th' wore spells, them words –
The map an' the key tae the treasure hoard.
Noo gi' us the marks for t' finnd 'em ageyn;
Howway doon t' the chorchyard an' ask the aa'd men,

For it's come wi' the wund an' gan wi' the wetter –
We'll noe be wantin' 'em noo...

But t' heor 'em gollerin' ower a boat
Wi' the soonds a the Norsemen still thick i' theer throat –
For' carlin t' fishroom, inwaver t' crook,
Ye'll nivvor finnd these i' the page on a beuk –
Ah, but they're bonny, the pairts on a cowble –
Dip a' the forefoot, lang i' the scorbel,
For' tack hyeuk an' gripe t' the horns a' hor scut,
For hor thofts t' hor thowelds – th' had nyems for the lot
That unlocked a hyel world...

                              – Which is no t' forgit
The fagarrashin foond in a fisherman's hut –
(Ye'd say it could dae wi' a reight reed up!) –
Wi' pellets an' dookas an' pickets an' poys,
Swulls an' sweels an' bows for buoys,
Rowells an' bowelts an' barky sneyds,
The tyeble aa' claed wi' perrins a' threed,
Wi' hoppin's an' hingin's tha's toozled like tows,
An' pokes for the whullicks, an' bundles a skowbs,
An' cloots for' a dopper the caaldies ha' chowed.

But hey – look oot! – divvin't gan in theer:
Ye'll nivvor git lowsed, 'cos she's wizenbank fair!

It aa' tummels oot in a roosty shoower;
The nets unraffle wi' cloods a stoor.
Ye're varnigh scumfished afore ye can caal
For the becket, the brailor, the ripper an' aa'
The whuppin's an' leashin's aback a the waa' –
By, lad, she's a reight Taggarine-man's haal!

An' it's nae bother – it's naen –
T' shut the door on yon.
Put oot the light. Forgit the nyems,
We'll nivvor be wantin' them things ageyn –
It's come wi' the wund an' gan wi' the wetter –
We'll noe be needin' 'em noo...

Aye, for warse or for better, w've aal had enyeugh:
Getten clear a the aa'd days – hard work, an' gey rough;
An' for nowt. But a lifetime is aa' that it's tyaen
T' git stowed oot wi' gadgets an' hoy oot wor brains;
Wi' sonar an' radar an' traals that'll gan
Ower fool groond an' fest'ners an' fetch up the spaa'n
Till there's nowt left t' catch but a roosty tin can.
An' by th' aa'd chorchyard, wor bairns wait at morn
On the skyul bus t' tyek 'em t' toons wheer th'll lorn
A mair wonders on orth than th' aa'd'uns had hord,
An' forgit aa' yon hand-me-doon rubbish an' words.

An' whils' they're away, the west wund cracks
As the Cheviot torns for' white t' black,
An' away up country, the sair-bittled land –
Blinkbonny, Blaawearie, Blin'born, Beefstand,
Bloodybush Edge – borsts intae spring
Wheer wor forefatthers fit. An' the reivin' wund
Carries the scent a the heather an' whins.
Aye, mebbes its reight t' forgit them things...

T' forgit...But what dae w' wekken t' finnd?
Darse, w're aal Europeans noo! – nivvor mind
That wor fatthers got lost gannin' sooth a the Tyne...
Whae, let's hoy oot the words wi' the work. What's the use
On a lingo like wors, that th' canna jaloose
In London, an' Brussels, an' places like yon?
But ye'd think w' wore aa' bairns, the way th' gan on –
For ye maa'n no dae this, an' ye canna dae thon,
An' aa' the smaa' fish ye hoy back at the sea –
They're 'Endangered Species! Set them free!'
– Fine words. Divvin't tell 'em the buggers aa' dee.

Noo fine words catch nae haddocks an' lengthen nae days:
What ye want is the words that are fit for y' ways,
For we're no aa' the syem. But th' come for' the toons,
An' ye meight as weel taalk t' the man i' the moon,
For the wull a the mony's a terrible thing:
We'll be aa' like the hedgehogs an' wake up in spring.
While the foreign boats come an' th' dae what th' like,
The toonies yap on, an' th'll tell ye what's reight
An' th' kna aa' the answers, an' hevvn't a clue –
An' whae's th' Endangered Species noo?

An' wull th' ax us what t' dae? Aye, wull they!
'Cos we divvin't speak reight – so th' say:
It's 'Ee kna nowt, ee herrods an' hinds...'
By, lad, but th' maa'n hae a deal on their minds
T' think like a dogger, man, aal askew;
An' Aah'll tell ye somethin', an' that's not two,
Theer's noo much wetter gans ower theer heeds –
They'd dae little for God if the divvil was deed.

But it's nae bother at aa'
T' set the bleeze away –
Stoke the fire, lads. See hor born –
Whoosh! Y' bugger, th've nowt t' lorn;
What th' cannot write an' th' divvin't speak
Gans up forivvor. The lowes an' reek
A' the maps an' the tunes an' the sangs an' the soonds
Are a hyel muckle library brunt t' the groond:
Aa' that w' wore an' aal w' kna
Come wi' the wund an' gan wi' the wetter.

Wad ee say that it mattered? Ye'll no can tell
Hoo the blethor w' blaa' is wor sense a worsells,
Wi' the soonds a the words like a dance i' the haal
Tiv an aa'd-farrened piper, wi' steps that w've aal
Putten lang oot a mind. Ye can say what ye like,
Whils' th' aa'd world gans back like the snaa' off a dyke,
Ye can hev your tongue scraped, but them words are no deed,
For th' rive at the hairs on the back a yeer heed.

The clarty words an' claggy words,
The carra-paa'd an' glaikit words:
Hurpellin', durrellin',
Haygellin', hurrellin',
Sneukin', plowtin',
Boolin', lowpin',
Scrafflin', wallerin', danderin' doon...

For there's words that'll lowp wi' a lollupin' tune,
Tha' can paint ye a pict'er, clear as noon.
Aah doobt th' could gi' a caa'driff tiv a styen,
Some a them words – th' can chill your byens:
A bleary wund, lad, bleachin' snaa' –
There's nae other soond for it. What wad ee caa'

Thon scaa'din', starvin' sooth-east blaa'
If she wasn't a Piner? Thon Gurrelly torn?
Yon sair Black Barber? A Hashy morn?
Can ye no feel the whup a the caa'd i' them soonds?
For wor words is wor eeyes an' wor lugs. I' the toons,
I' the skyuls, on the T.V., Aah doobt but ye'll finnd
What brings far worlds nigh-handed maa'n leave ee for blinnd.

Daresay, mebbes ye'll no tyek much heed on your borth:
We maa'n be like the mowldies that howk i' th' orth
Wi naen eeyes an' nae words. For hoo can w' tell
Of a hobble, a range, or a rowelly sweel,
Or a little bit lipper that breks on the beach
Wi' the flood a' the tide, if w' hevvn't the speech?

Noo w're far for' them things; an' wor bairns divvin't kna
A field set wi' kyel for' the bagie shaa's,
An' theer isn't a job t' be had heor aroond,
An' the words divvin't fit when th' get t' the toons.
For the graith a them words are reight heor wheer th' grew
I' the land an' the sea, an' th' divvin't allow
For the way that the toons ha' stapped up the springs
T' the truth a wor hairts an' the meanin's a things.

Noe, Aah wadn't gan back t' the past. But Aah'd say,
Noo machines dae the work, when w' moved t' the sway
O' the orth an' the sea, bi the cowble an' ploo,
W' wore fuller wi' sommat w're hunger't for noo.
True nowth. It's the beat a the words i' the blood;
Like the sap a' the spring i' the black esh bud,
Like the dishalagie-leaves on the banks a the born,
Or the boontree bush proggin' the thick a the thorn,
Or a muckle grut thrussel that borsts through the corn
Like a neeve – th've a life on theer aa'n. Aye –

Come wi' the wund an' gan wi' the wetter,
Born 'em! Hoy 'em away! – Nae matter,
Them words boonce back wi' one hell of a clatter…
W've seen it aal afore.
Put oot the light. Forgit the nyems,
We'll nivvor be wantin' them words ageyn –
But wunds that hurpel oot the day
Can hurrel in the morn':

Fit as a linty, quick an' clivvor
Like the grilse that breests the river
Heedin' hyemward, or the ether
Wha shifts his shape amang the heather,
Th' torn wi' th' yeor,
Wi' the light, wi' the weather –
Foller the sun, the rain – whativvor
Stors on the hills, i' the hyem, i' the hairt,
Comes wi' the wund an' gans wi' the wetter...

The Blue Lonnen

The crunch of mussel shells under the boot heel;
The bramble-patch where the cottages were rooted;

The stone ring of the mussel bed, the stair
To the drying-green, the ballast heap, the beach of creeve-stones;

The tarry stain where the bark-pot reeked; the wicket
In the wall; on the bridge to the limpets, the blade-worn groove;

The iron pin that marks the sea-road to the haven;
The nail driven into the door jamb – they are illegible

Without the rudder and the anchor,
Without the twine, the needle and the knitter:

For these are the paths they beat to the shore – The Nick. The Blue Lonnen –
And each is a road with a boat at the end of it.

How the Coble Came to Be

The sea made it. First
Its cold, salt draw-knife
Scoured the sky

Over Ross Sands and Fenham
Till it was clean,
A pure edge. Then

It carved out dunes –
Curves, as if land
Were like it. The wind

Whipped up a storm:
Two-thousand wings,
One heart, beating.

Next, it twisted
An auger through Budle:
The scream of a curlew.

Then out of the blue
Eye of the North Sea, its roll,
Its corkscrew swell,

Out of its craggy vowels –
Skeer, Carr, Steel –
Its guts between rocks –

From the precise curve
Of the cormorant's dive,
The sheer of its beak,

The hunter's lean line;
Out of the cuddy duck's
Broad beam, buoyant –

From this exact
Collusion of opposites –
From the sea that joined

And the sea that separates –
Onto the miles of sand
The first boat landed.

The Bonny Boat

Has she got a good high heed, your boat?
Is she laid-in right?
Does she look weel? Or does she coower hor heed, hor starn
Cocked up aheight?

An' has she got a right dip gripe, yon boat?
Does she draa' plenty watter?
Them modern boats, the heeds just blaa's awa'.
The forefoot winna haa'd hor.

So ha' ye got two masts aboard your boat
An' your lang tiller?
An' is your pitch-pine ruther dip withaa'
So ye can sail hor?

An' ha' ye got a right peak on your sail?
Your mast raked back?
Nowth-country boats could dae hor, lad.
One tack

For' Beadlin up t' Amble. O, a bonny boat
Will aye gan weel.
There's varnigh not a bonny boat been built
That winna sail.

Building the Boat

First comes the dance of nails.
Oak crook and larch –
Ram-plank and stem-post, scarphed,

And the planks slowly flowering outwards
From nothing
But the idea of rightness.

Like water, the grain
Flows and the plank bends:
Nothing forced or steamed.

From their grown shape
Arches the strength of each timber,
Each supple plank.

The boat-builder's measured eye
Judges. He is listening.
Composer of silence,

He does not make this tune,
But follows the line
To its natural conclusion

With draw-knife, chisel, hammer,
Smoothed by countless palms,
Father, son; with names –

Inwaver. Sewin'-nail. Drowt –
Planed by a thousand voices,
Shaping a dark procession.

The new boat waits.
Shored up with blocks,
Amphibian legs, it stands

Balanced on the brink
Of memory and future,
Poised, ready to move

From thought to wood to water.

Cathy

'See yon hyeuk?' says Cathy.
'Yon's ma life.'
Three-quarters of an inch of steel,

Barbed at the hyeutter, bent,
It glitters
Like a jewel.

Tiny. Cathy, six stone, volatile as petrol,
Wiry, lean,
Puts on her shawl.

Pleased to see you, kettle on,
Deaf as a sharpening stone
To every sound

Except the wireless static crackle
From the boat,
A little whirlwind,

She pegs the sheets out in the back yard,
Scrubs the step, stirs the pan,
Swabs the floor:

'When fetther hord it was
Another girl
He slammed the door.

Aye, but
He couldn't dae wi'oot dowters, ye kna.'

Cathy, bent
Beneath the creel:
Home from the mussel beds, the limpet pool;

Six stone of haddocks haa'ked aroond Reed Raa',
Husband, in-laws, tugging at her, kin
Needing her care,

Mussels to skeyn,
The boat to launch, lines to bait, claes to poss,
Sons to bear;

Cathy, bent with pains,
Years; busy as a sanderling,
Never still,

Down the harbour with the barrow, eyes
Blue as the Coquet, bright
As steel,

As hard, as sharp, as necessary
As a fish-hook
To the house, the men;

Cathy, without whom
A coble could not go to sea – as vital to it
As diesel, or the wind.

Boulmer Tractors

These Boulmer tractors – Zetor, Fordson Major –
Strong as lions, rusted, scabbed and holed,

Their four-square iron shoulders hunched, are waiting
Here, on the winter beach, at the edge of the world

Where the reefs lie horizontal to the shore –
The North Reins, the South Reins, Marmouth Scars –

A ruled line. A wall. This is the end,
This village with no shop, no bus. The wind

Scours down the road where every door is shut,
As if everyone here had grown too old, worn out

From staring east, from watching for the men
To steam into sight like spring with their boxes of salmon.

The next stop is a Conservation Zone –
Tractors, trailers, tidied away. Gone

Over to nature, if anyone knew what that meant.
The tractors wait for a movement order. Then,

Though their exhausts are blown, their tyres bald,
Like the great-grandmothers of men, in ragged shawls,

Straining every muscle, two abreast,
Heaving the coble up the beach, stern first,

Stoic, relentless, inch by inch – they will
Judder to life and, roaring, smoking, wheels

Flinging up rotten weed, salt spray and stones,
Rise from the sea, and haul the last boat home.

Family

Tonight, within sound of the sea, a man, no longer young,
Is getting ready for bed. Before dawn
He will slip out between black piers, alone.

He has three hundred creeves to haul: too many.
The diesel that Fastworker burns, no other way
To make a living, but by hammering the sea.

It's not what he would choose. Nearby, the old boat
Loosens slowly, nail by nail, opening out.
He is both sorry and not sorry to see her go.

There are few people left in the village who understand this:
She is more than a boat. She is a window
Back to where he came from. She is family.

Before he sleeps, he takes a breath. Tomorrow
Is forecast fair, there's not much wind. Along the row
A blackbird calls; and others echo, echo.

No One Said a Word

Off Howdiemont, the sea grows pale.
The sky turns silver-pink. The pools

Brim with light. The oystercatcher
Yelps, the turnstones rise, and over

The North Bay, the red sun flares.
It floods the holes, the Iron Skeers,
The bents, the Bathing House, the wares,

Without a sound. At the Weir Buses,
At Hip's Heugh on the Hinds' Hooses,

Not a single boat. No yellow figure
Squints, beatified, his fingers

Coiling the wet tow, lacing the creeves.
No wake of white gulls ploughs the sea.

No boot-sole prints the soft mud track
To Sugar Sands; and down the rocks

No woman bends her shadowy
Four-footed shape at Shallowarry.

The seas break on the Big Skeer,
Slowly roll over, a distant roar,

A taste of iron. A knotted hawser
Twists, a frozen current of water.

Split like an oak-stump, ten feet tall,
Riveted with barnacles,

The great pipe-organ boiler towers.
The seas around it blossom, flower,

Over and over. No one mourns
The countless quiet men and women

Who softly shuffled from this shore,
Their limpet creels, their swulls, their gear,

Their heavy hearts. No, no one heard
Them leave. Nobody said a word.

Plenty Lang a Winter

Howway doon the harbour.
Gan off afore the dawn —
Plenty lang a winter
T' lay abed aa' morn.

Plenty lang a winter,
Naen salmon i' the bay,
An' lang eneugh asleep, lad,
When your livin's rived away;

When your livin's rived away, lad,
An' the big man greeds your keep.
Plenty lang a winter.
Lang eneugh asleep.

Alnmouth

Something unassuageable about an estuary.
Black ooze, oily,

Clinging. Dragging east,
Miles of cloud rubble.

Acres of sea-purslane.
Redshank, dunlin,

Camouflaged. Dissemblance.
Chains of footprints

Snaking through mud. Loops
Of old rope. A curlew

Letting go its rinsed notes.
Abandonment.

And, slowly filling with water,
A boat

Rotten beyond rescue, its anchor-chain
Stiff; paint, lichen,

Flaking from its timbers, revealing
Strong, clear lines. What matters

Is sunk, uncovered
And sunk. On the far bank, a train,

A straight line on the heugh,
Hauling its troubles south.

And between them, the river
Slipping from green fields, Scots pines, gables –

Pink, blue, terracotta –
From the gull-squabble,

Towards something sparer:

Wormcasts.
Ripples.

On the far side of the water,

Walls, roofless.
Gleaming bent-grass.

Its surface wind-hatched, stippled with light,
The river

Is letting go
At the end of its life, an old man

Catching sight of what matters –
That muffled roar,

The stern white line of the breakers.

The Old Boat

The old boat stands on the bank-top.
Long stains of rust
Run from her scut-irons, beadings. Daylight
Gleams through her rents.

Grass grows around her. Sparrows
Forage in the dry weed.
'A little worm has getten in ablow the scowbels,'
Billy said

Last winter. So they towed her onto the bank
And left her there
Like an old woman who has lost her reason,
Staring

Blankly at the sea, while the paint peels back:
The grain appears
In swirls and eddies, as if slowly
Returning to the tree;

Though still the straight planks fan
In their lovely curve, the flow
And figure-eight she makes – the geometry of beauty
Last to go.

They were hoping for a miracle.
That, half a century
After the first-clenched nail, Hector would fettle her.
But the years were too many.

This winter, nobody speaks of her.
No one can bear
To smash her up. To burn her. She is the sewing-nail
That holds them there.

She is the last link of the chain
That stretches away to sea, to the horizon.
She is the ruled line.
The end of the line.

Without her
There is no reason.

Sea, Sky, Stars

Cold tonight. No moon. The frost
Crackles on limestone. I'm staring east

From Beadnell Point beneath a sky
So starry, it steals my breath away;

North, to the Plough, and near the horizon,
Saturn, Sirius, Orion.

I'm trying to name them: the Byre-End Hard,
The Benty Smooth and the Barnyards –

The constellations of known ground.
Hills, hollows, rocks, sand.

Knot by knot, they wove that net,
Charlie, Billy, Ree'ford, bent

Each to the next men's ground, the next,
To Craster Smooth, Boulmer Sooth Hard,

To Cars'well Skeers, and south. Their marks,
Their grid of bearings, like the stars –

Not just a map, but a mesh of stories –
Lit up where and what we are.

Silence. The ebb's hush. What sails on
In us the sea will take, and soon

The dark, the stars. The grains of sand
Are not more numerous. This land,

The fields, the continents, pegged out
Across the surface of the planet,

Less dense, less populous than this
Black sea, starry and fathomless.

5

COAL ROADS

The Dark Passages

I

I said to the stars:
  What is written
  Down in the dark,
  In the dark passages?

From the space at Nothing's heart
North and South were wrenched apart.

Out in the dark, the farthest stars
Stamp their braille that no one reads:
A message sent and not received.

In the ear the waves of sound
Roll like breakers up the sand
From the time when time began.

There are rocks and there are rivers
  But at last
  All rocks are rivers.

The singing grass and the aching sky
Are waves that break upon the eye.

In the book of sperm and blood
Are written the recipes of the dead.

The equivocation of the North
Records the story of the Earth.

I said to the stars:
  What is written
  Down in the dark,
  In the dark passages?

II *Song of the Dead Men*

We are the Deed Men, drillin' the foreheed,
Brekkin' the deed grund, drivin' the levels.
> *Brae the mell an' torn a quatter.*
> *Brae mell. Brae.*

Winnin' the hard grund, we are the Deed Men
Blastin' black poother, breathin' the stoor in.
> *Brae the mell an' torn a quatter.*
> *Brae mell. Brae.*

We are the Deed Men, drivin' the levels,
Spar t' the dump an' bouse t' the kibbles.
> *Brae the mell an' torn a quatter.*
> *Brae mell. Brae.*

Deed grund won, lads, breathin' black stoor in.
Hard life, hard deeth. We are the Deed Men.
> *Brae the mell an' torn a quatter.*
> *Brae, brae, brae.*

III *Song of the Bouse*

Forst t' the knockstone t' brae us b' hand,
Then t' the rollers t' crush us t' sand.
Next Aah'll be sieved on the trammel for fines,
Then t' the hotchin' tub – jig oot the slimes.
The sludge fr' the buddle is weshed b' the born
An' as smiddum Aah'll bleeze i' the mill fires the morn'.

There are rocks and there are rivers
> *But at last*
> *All rocks are rivers.*

IV *The Smiddy Widow*

Let the rock sweat its drops of lead,
Let them sink through the cinders;
Let a blast from the bellows fire his face blood-red;
Let the heat skin his eyes, sting his cheeks; let him choke
On the brimstone stink as he rakes through the slag.
What pools in the sumpter stiffens in the pigs.
What is scraped from the chimney settles in the blood.
It's a sky-high price, this almost-irredeemable
Mineral purity, this slippery, equivocal
Melt of rock and flux of lead.
It's a hex. It's a curse. It's some other hand's work,
What fires wrought, gasping through cracks in the thin earth.

Sedimentary

This is a layered landscape,
Scarred
And heaved wide open to reveal
Its inmost part,
The cumulative quick of its
Recording heart.

Tumultuous and barren,
It lies hacked
Or hollowed; age on age,
Its history stacked
In horizontal bands of grey and ochre,
Cracked

By deep descending fissures
Reaching down
Into the lightless crunch of dense
Compacted stone,
The graveyard of lost continents
Remade as one.

Here, ferns and forests, and inhabitants of oceans,
Dumb and blind,
Have found themselves unstrung, and slowly
Redefined
As grit beneath the fingertips.
Through time,

The dust of distant planets
Knits in scars
With all the creeping, quivering things
That seed and spark
And tremble on the edge of life like the
Remotest stars.

Out of the Dark

Out of the dark
    Came heat and light.

How far, how deep
    Are the workings that made us?

    As deep as remembering.
    As far as tomorrow.

On Seaham Headland

I

Rock
Is a cold document.

Our lives, too,
A line of sediment.

II

Beneath the fields, a forest
Of fallen bones.

Listen:
Our prayers whisper in the long grass.

III

Rich, we possessed
The gold horizon.

What lasts,
But the waves will break it?

IV

The blacksmith has hammered a blade
And the mason, a hand.

Stone hand, bless
Hands that are frail and warm.

V

A road to the sea, a hearth
And a driftwood fire:

Pilot, where are the marks
To guide us home?

Roads

(after George Mackay Brown)

I

To the landsman,
The gull-roads are ways to the sea,
To the sailor, roads to the land.

II

Road of fish-hook and creel,
Driftwood, sea-coal,
Burnt lime, salt and ale:
These are the roads to the shore.

III

The sea itself is a road,
Oar and sail
Bringing strange tongues, coins, blood,
Taking
Grain, coal, sons.

IV

The burns gush, the trees shiver.
The dene is a green road the red fox travels.

V

The roads they hacked and drilled
From the roots of dead forests,
Under the fields of corn,
Under the sea to the horizon,

Are nothing now but stories.

VI

Carbon-black, the sky
Above the headland
Is lit with the routes of stars:
Where we came from.

VII

Along such roads
We carry all we have:
Memory. Hope. Love. –

Show us the road into the future.

The Rooks

The rooks of St Mary's Churchyard are massing for evening.
From the sycamores of Lord Byron's Walk they rise
In raucous, wheeling clouds, then swirl and settle
Out of the sky.

How quietly the gold creeps into the barley
Evening by evening. How quickly the dust begins to fall.
How soon a straight back stiffens, a voice weakens,
While the rooks call,

Call. Witnesses to Londonderry's riches,
To the town's prosperity and the pitman's graft –
Those dark tides of sons and fathers, leaving, returning
From the pit shaft,

Unstoppable as the sea – they are onlookers
To great catastrophes: wars, strikes; to private hearts
Smashed like pebbles in the wreck of wave and water.
The flock flies apart.

Something has broken it: but only for a moment.
Over the black treetops it turns like a wheel
As it always has – as it did when Dawdon and Seaham
Were barley fields;

And falling and rising again, a single being
Drawn together out of dark and dust, it will be the same
A thousand years from now, when Seaham and Dawdon
Are only names.

Lost Names

Pond Garth . Low Garth . Glebe Land . Lint Links .
Eleven Score Riggs . The Flower Field . Yeland .
Bowes . Milbanke . Byron . Vane Tempest .
Londonderry . Hewer . Putter . Stoneman . Filler .
Teamer . Trimmer . Oystercatcher . Turnstone .
Skylark . Redshank . Periwinkle . Sea Anemone .
The Excelsior . The Livingstone . The Norman .
The Bee . The Cornucopia . The Lady Ann .

Wheel

I

By these whins
   and that wall,
By this broken cliff
   and that path,
Sycamore, elm
   and the sky, be witness

To the infinite within us.

From the famed
   to the forgotten,
From the old men
   to the children,
From the coal roads
   to the rock rose:

We are one wheel.

II

Fire in the blood,
Fire in the grave,
Green fire in the leaf:
  Turn, wheel

Iron-fire, glass-fire,
Brick-fire, black fire,
Fire in the furnace:
  Turn, wheel

What is life but a fuel for burning,
Change, returning
Old for new?
  Turn, wheel

Lost Paths

Lame old man who walks these lanes –
The cart tracks, the corn paths,

White roads of salt and milk,
Tracks of the tale-teller and the news-bringer;

Who follows the pointing fingers of hawthorn,
Old before the pits were sunk,

Down the Black Path, the Nannygoat's Path,
Petwell Lonnen, Fillpoke –

Why do you keep walking?
Is it to forget

The miles of drowned roads down below,
The coal roads' narrowness?

As if you could tramp them away,
Blow off the memory

In the drifts of cow-parsley, in the garlicky dene,
Up Beacon Hill, ablaze with whins,

On the road with the sea at the end of it,
A sheet of light in the wind;

As if you could leave them behind –
Keep one step ahead of that sound –

The buzz in your head, in your bones, your blood,
That any day now will command you

Back underground.

Roads Out of Nowhere

These three are sorcerers, conjuring
Roads out of nowhere:

Tommy of White Lea, high on his tractor,
Drawing a gull-road over the loam;

The Julie Ann, with her box of blue lobsters,
Ploughing behind her a white road of foam;

And high above Blackhall banks, the skylark,
Spooling his thread,

Undoing the dark roads under the sea, and freeing
Summer ahead.

The Blast

Half a mile above the pit
The sea flings its guts
Back at the shore:
Tubes, belts, cables.

Forgetting
Is a slow rust.

The ghost-grey cliffs
Bare their scars to the light,
And the sea that made and unmakes them
Lays down
Its latest tribute:

Half-remembered, half-heard
On the empty air, the old voices
Work their way out of the shale:

An extinct species.

The Pitman's Boot

Breaks out of the shale like a fossil:

Black wrack clings to it.
Fine silt pours from it.
Dull fires gnaw at it.
Sea-salt stiffens it.

Ringed with the grain of water,
Shedding
Skin, scales, steel toe
Curled like a cod's lip, it gapes

Astonished

At its own survival.

The Pigeon Men

Three men are leaning on the corrugated iron,
Staring out across the fields at the china blue
Stretch of sky beyond. They are waiting for something.
'Ye couldn't buy that view,'

Kit shakes his head. His son John reaches up on tiptoe,
A little apart, on the loft roof, watching. Their backs
Are turned to the hand-stitched patchwork of crees, sheds, fences,
The secret shacks

And small doors cobbled from sleepers and iron sheeting
Hauled up from underground. It was pit-work
That made them ache to be out here in the sunshine
Among the birds.

'See yon green fields? Yonder's where Horden pit was –
The biggest pit in Europe, that. Nowt there now. Gone.'
John bites his tab, says nothing; glares into the distance.
Then he throws up his white dove like a flag: 'Come on!'

And suddenly the sky is full of pigeons.
Over Blackhills Dene and Paradise they fly –
Places that are names on the map now only:
Warren House, Whiteside,

And Clifton, Coxon, Cuba Streets – the vanished
Homes of vanished men who never dreamed
How much of themselves they nailed in the crees and gardens.
Home the birds stream,

While John, on the stock-loft roof, waves the frantic fantail.
'Come on!' he yells to the open sky: 'Howway!'
And the white wings beat at the end of his outstretched fingers,
As if he too was ready to fly away.

Turning the Tide

The beach is a box of jewels; scraps
Of green and amber Candlish glass
Flicker and glint where the salty foam
Fizzes on flint and fiery stones.
Featherbed Rock. Bessy's Hole.

The cliffs are made of soft, white cheese.
They crumble to the touch. The sea
Has swallowed all the evidence
Of yesterday, its brilliance
Itself a kind of alchemy.

What is this coast? Horizon. Strand
With no beginning and no end,
A line, rewritten hour by hour,
The tale we tell about ourselves.

Riddle of the skylark, hiss of the sea:
Who, on the river of cars that sweeps
Past Seaham Harbour, out of reach,
Has time to listen before he sleeps?
Nannygoat's Path. Frenchman's Creek.

At Nose's Point, the round rolled bricks,
Londonderry-stamped, have lost
Their letters, and all names are dust:
The Flower Field. The Ballast Beach.

Horses on the hillside, skewbald galloways,
Knee-deep in dockens, chew on their memories;
Chum'uns, full'uns, down the long wagonways.

Red Shale boulders down The Blast,
Sea-built speckled cliffs of waste;
Waves have sorted, hand over hand,
The iron-oxide raddled bands,
Purple ash, fool's gold and grey,
Sticky, kaolin-like clay:
What we discard, the sea redeems
In imitation of its own

Volcanic outpourings and slow
Imprisonments in beds of stone.

Here lie fossils, classified
In the museum of the tide,
Unseen, unvisited: bones, guts
Of great endeavours; bolts, nuts,
Cables, roof-props, transport-belts;

And trapped and mangled in between,
A dinosaur – some vast machine –
Crushed in sludge; from whence the waves
Now liberate a boot, a blade,
A pick, a glove, a grey string vest,
A pony's breast-plate – forlorn ghosts.
Things men worked with their bare hands,
Strewn in silence on the sand,
Hold their spirit in them still.
Hawthorn. Blue House. Beacon Hill.

Beyond the yellow slopes of whin
Rooks rise up, and silver-green
Meadow grasses hush and sway
From Durham City, worlds away.
Tier on tier, the steep ravines,
Eagle Hall, Hawthorn Dene,
Stitched like veins through time, still hide
All their secrets deep inside;

And looking back, down canopies
Of dark, impenetrable trees
That close upon the depths below,
And out, across the fields that blow
For miles, towards the shining sea
Before you, you could never guess
How history closes over us
Like water, healing its own skin.
Five Quarter, Hutton and Low Main.

Blossom on the coal-black railway track;
Sweet white hawthorn, dandelion, dock,
Whose is the hand turns back the clock?
The Canch. The Facin'. Cinderella Rock.

145

The railway line holds back a tide
Of settlement, a sea of lives
Contained in regimented rows
Of slate-grey roofs and brick-red homes
That, only a century ago,
Were farms, and fields, and quiet lanes.
Withering Hope. Foxholes Dene.

The wheel turns quickly. Kittiwakes
Clamour in the rocky nooks,
And all along the Grassy Banks –
The Tatie Hole. The Boatie Bay –
Skylarks weave and cowslips shiver,
And something has been lost forever.

'Muck means jobs.' That paradox
Blackened the sand from Seaham Docks
And Hawthorn Hive and Horden Dene
To Crimdon. Now the beach is clean.

And Easington and Horden lie
Smokeless beneath an open sky.
The pigeons wheel above. On red
Back lanes of shale, by tatie beds,
And barking dogs and coops and crees,
Men bite their tongues; stare out to sea.

Spring Bank, Moorstack, Fiery Hill;
Warren House. Whitesides Gill.

On Horden's platform of grey ash
Prehistoric, smoky grass
Whispers to the desert shore:
Stones and silence. Nothing more.
Out of the blue, a turnstone cries.
Acid pools give back the sky:
Reflect the fate of all we build.
Aerial Flight. Limekiln Gill.

Where the eerie Dene Mouth spills
Its vegetable green, and swills
The rubble on the beach ahead –
The stones, a dried-blood, burnt-brick red –

The viaduct's massive columns rise,
Slender as trees, cathedral-high,
And make nine windows of the sky.

Here, with every step, you meet
The charred, black relics of defeat.
The waves are hissing in the bay;
The rancid taste won't wash away
On any tide. Along this coast
Forgetting is a long, slow rust.

Iron in the rammel, fire in the soul:
This is the coast where men won coal;
Loved it, loathed it, lived and died
To keep those fires alight. The tide
Put them out, but they're burning still.
Black Hall. Fillpoke. Bluehouse Gill.

What is this coast? The tale we tell
About ourselves. The visible
Reminder of the levelling
Of water everywhere. The line
Of the horizon. The great chain
Of carbon: smoking rock, and rain,
And coral, dying into stone,
And fallen forests, crushed to coal.
It measures us. While lives, like light
On water, glimmer and go out,
Still, with every breaking wave,
The sea gives back its tale – that change
Is all there is. That we arrive
And leave on these indifferent tides.

At Blackhall Rocks, the children play
Oblivious among the caves.
Between the footprints that they leave
And the water's edge, all love,
All fears are lodged. In such small boats
We place our lorryloads of hope.

The white gulls wheel against the sun.
Embedded in the banks lie bone
Arrow-heads and skeletons.

Beneath the children's footprints run
The great drowned roads beneath the sea.

It lies beyond imagining,
That history of fire within,
Binding the heart to the broken rock.
The children laugh behind The Stack.
Greenstairs. Gin Cave. Dead Man's Bank.
The shore lies silent, a closed book
They have not read. Their futures stretch
Ahead of them along the beach.

6

HALIWERFOLK

Durham Cathedral

Imagine it a ruin.
A spot-lit arch. Its towers
Toppled. The river
Kerving a jud

In the fading light
At the thin end of the year.
Though its countless sockets
Hold a darkness – ours –

In Elvet, North Bailey,
Cobbled Owengate,
Rising, fugitive
As coal smoke on the breath,

From knotwork on vellum,
Keel, scroll, laced
Branches or, beneath,
From a blacker seam –

Hyeven, Hinny, Hyem –
The old words loom,
High, mysterious,
Lit up from within.

Holy Island Arch

Against the buffeting wind and the sea's growl
The crafted stone
Soars overhead in the high blue forever,
Thin as a wishbone.

Nothing so fragile should stand so strong.
Leaping, unbound,
As if quarried blocks were weightless; as if wind
Could not suddenly dash them down,

The sandstone balanced by the mason's hand
Impossibly, holds.
All grace defies weight, logic, weather –
Bends, a bow –

Hope, launching itself
Into cold space.
The breaking sun transfigures it. An equal,
Opposite embrace

Is all that keeps the stones from crashing,
And the heart,
That has one longing only – to be met and held
In such an arch.

Beach Ride

Throughout: sound recorded from horse galloping on sand; sea and birds.

As a prayer t' the wund,
As the dew t' the dawn,
As the day tae it's end,
As the prick a the thorn;

As the bend a the tide   Spindrift,
As the fresh a the born,   And the wind's drum –
As the airt a the wund,   Music, old
As the prick a the thorn;   As wonder and longing;

As the fresh a the born,   *Fly, foam.*
As the range a the sea,   *Flow, sea.*
As the bend a the tide,   *Sweep, wind.*
As the spuggie maa'n flee.   *Foam, flee.*

    Give the horses their heads now: *Fly, foam.*
    Let them fly,   *Flow, sea.*
    Foam flecks blown   *Sweep, wind.*
    From that first, lost sea;   *Foam, flee.*

As the bend a the tide,   Spindrift,
As the fresh a the born,   And the wind's drum –
As the airt a the wund,   Music, old
As the prick a the thorn;   As wonder and longing;

As the fresh a the born,   *Fly, foam.*
As the range a the sea,   *Flow, sea.*
As the bend a the tide,   *Sweep, wind.*
As the spuggie maa'n flee.   *Foam, flee.*

    Waves, hooves,   *Lash, wind.*
    And a cave-fire story,   *Tear, mane.*
    River of sand   *Hoof, nostril,*
    Flowing under us, tell   *Flare, flame.*

    How they stream headlong,   *Fly, foam.*
    The minutes, the dear ones,   *Flow, sea.*
    Love to its end,   *Sweep, wind.*
    Time to its stillness.   *Foam, flee.*

When the Tide Comes In

A poem for two voices and a chorus

First voice:
Softly, across the sweep of sand
The tide
Eases in on the unwary traveller
From the southern side.

Under a windy sky, invisibly, the water dawdles,
Flows
Into the Black Burn, the Stinking Gut,
Silent, and slow.

Newsreader (second voice):
A reminder of the News Headlines:
A group of Civil Liberties protesters has been arrested outside a Summit of European Ministers on Tyneside. 70 EU Ministers were attending the Summit on Counter-terrorism.

The Home Secretary announced today that students will be encouraged to apply for identity cards from 2010. Private firms will be supported in an initiative to set up 'biometric enrolment centres', where ID card applicants will be fingerprinted and information collected for the National Identity Register.

And finally:
A family has been rescued off a tidal causeway in Northumberland after their estate-car was washed out to sea while they were asleep. The causeway, which connects Holy Island to the mainland, is covered twice a day by the sea. The driver and his wife and their two children had parked and fallen asleep on Monday night, thinking that they were on the other side of the causeway. The Seahouses lifeboat and an RAF helicopter found the car floating out to sea. All four occupants were waving from the roof.

First voice:

Chorus:
Security,
Security,
Security,
Security...

Second voice:

Over the miles, unseen, the water idles,
Creeps;

DNA database, CRB Checks,
CCTV,

From Cockly Knowes streams north
to Goswick sands.
It seeps

Civil Contingencies, Stop-and-Search,
On-the-Spot-
Fines,

Up through the mud; the trickles quicken
while, heedless,
We sleep.

Parenting Order, Control Order,
Antisocial Behaviour
Order,

Then from the Foolwork Burn, the Swad,
The Batt,

Serious Organised Crime and Police
Act,

Across the oyster scarp and sand-eel beds,
The eel-grass flats

Criminal Justice and Public Order
Act,

Where white knots twist against the windy sky,
It builds, and bursts

Legislative and Regulatory Reform
Act;

Into the torrent of the Low
And Gut
That meet, and merge; till,
like a lock, the sea
Snaps shut!

Security, Security,
Security, Security,
Surveillance, Surveillance,
Save us!
Save us!

Surveillance, Surveillance,
Surveillance, Surveillance,
Compliance, Compliance,
Compliance!

154

Horizon

From the babe in arms
To the home for the elderly;

From the rock of faith
To the quicksand of anxiety;

From the open door
To the closed-circuit camera;

From the chain and anchor
To the far-flung flotsam;

From the slate
To the keyboard;

From the eye
To the echometer;

From the hobnail clatter
To the swish of tyres;

From the salt-tongued chatter
To the synthesised bleep

That repeats and repeats;
From the sea-coal fire

To the humming switch;
From the stitch in time

To the lorryloads of styrofoam
Stranded on the tideline –

Not what we own
But where we belong;

Not the mesh of the blood
But the net of our knowing;

Not what we buy
But what we become;

Not what is consumed
But what we keep building;

Not chiselled in rock
But carved in water

Between the printed sand
And the far horizon,

The deep we trawl,
The deep we cannot fathom,

Where we choose to sail
When we put out to sea.

Windmill Steads

Even after they left,
When strangers ripped the stones from its old walls, burned

Its roof-tree, oak
Stripped from a shipwreck, raised

Outside new, shiny sea-front homes,
Revetments for the sea to thump against,

What remained of its rooms –
Pulled inside out, crowded with sour nettles –
Hissed

Back at the white rigs, rip-tides, where
On east wind nights, the sea beat at the door,

The cradle rocked like a boat in the swell's back-draught.

Herring
Came and went. Houses.

Then the old ones, helpless,

Mouthed one last prayer against
The sea's indifference.

The Whale

That January, the sea brought us a message –
Monumental, big as a black bus, ribbed,
Rubbery, vulcanised, arched like a bridge,

There it lay one morning – a sperm whale,
Making for another world, and perished.

It looked old as the rock. It was mottled brick-red
And chalked pinkish-white, like a fresco
In a dark church. Its fluke was etched

Delicately greenish-pink; its side
Rose, a black slag-heap, a hill of cinders,
Red oxides, oily residues and clinker.

We were drawn to it. Huddled on the bank-top,
Facing the horizon, hunched against the wind
And cold, we stared and stared at it, in wonder.

Then the sea, with the noise of a great machine,
Rolled its dark bulk towards us and, graceful
As weed, it raised one flipper like a sign;

And the sea heaved; lifted its great weight, light
As a breath, or a gift – Here, take it.

The Refuge Box

I

Sound of Holy Island sands — wide, empty — spring, early morning, tide out.

At the edge of the Low, the wind blows cold.

A world that is water and not water
Stretches away, reticulate;

Shaken within it, redshank, godwit,
Their scraps and patches of safety shrinking,

Spreading. Miles of sand-flats. Glittering
Streams and ribbons of water, weaving

Earth and sky; between them, the golden
Island, afloat on equivocation,

Or safely grounded there, the tide
Either coming or going around it, the road

Snaking towards it, narrow, human.

Fade up seals, low Hooooo.

You reach the Danger sign, and stop.
You want it, that Island, stretched out like a ship

Ashore on its saltings, adrift in a sea
So blue and endless, you'd think the sky

Had swallowed it up, or else had fallen
Smack down into its own reflection.

Out from the causeway, over the sand,
Guideposts narrow towards the Island,

The mirror-image of their own
Vanishing — an invitation.

The Slakes answer the sky's question:

Blue?

  Blue.

    Now, will you

Step out into an unknown element?

              End seals.

Tick tock, tick tock,   *Cobwebs doon the lonnen,*
Hurryin', scurryin',
High wetter, low wetter,   *Blue lowes i' the fire,*
Spring come early,
Hour-glass, weather-glass,   *Black scum on the wetter,*
Berrellin', derrellin',
Tick tock, tick tock,   *Better watch the tide.*
Time runnin' oot.

Tentative, the tide, a feather,
Brushes the tarmac, skimming over;

Again, another – films of water
Lapping, crossing, catching hold,

Fizzing, creeping up the road,
An edge of paper, smouldering.

Ten minutes is all it takes.

Then, in the distance, the uncertain
Rattle of a motor. Idle,
Hesitating…

Creeping, seeping,
Icy, salty,
Softly, slowly,
Tortuous, sinuous,

Winding, twining,
Bitter, briny,
Seeping, creeping,
Infiltrating,

Steeping and
Insinuating,
Drenching, drowning,
Inundating.

Undercurrents. Tide-rips. Sudden
Snatching torrents. The road hidden

And, before you,
A small white shed on stilts.
A stairway.
A door.

Sound of feet on steps, door to Refuge Box, entering.

II

Summer, traffic, chatter, children.

An hour before the tide, the road
Is carnival, and miracle.

The ice-cream van, the picnic rugs,
The shrimping nets. A snake of cars

Breathes its heat-haze up the hill.

The ebb-tide tugs against the wind.
Trousers rolled, sandshoes in hand,

A straggle of visitors ventures out:
'Whoa! It's cold, man!' Hot, impatient,

The line of motors swelters, ticks,
Fumes at the sea's edge; and is still.

Skylarks on slacks; one at first, building up to the sound
they make out on the Swad – odd, eerie, multiple skylarks.

On the dry sand-slopes, the pale, neurasthenic
Lindisfarne helleborine

Shivers. High over his fiefdom –
Marram-grass, tarmac,

Bent-grass, milkwort, camper van, family saloon,
Marsh orchid and motorbike –
The skylark pours out his music,

At home in two elements,
Unseen;

And nobody speeding along the causeway hears him
Spinning his invisible threads between.

I am in flight
Away from it all. Away
From the wheel and the whirl of it,
From the can-you-just and the fax and the phone and the in-box,
From the treadmill, from the deadline, from the daily grind,
This wi-fi broadband mobile buzz –
It's an illness,
This noise in the head, this headlong race, this rush –
I am in flight, I am in search of

Stillness.

III

Summer sounds, St Cuthbert's Island, quiet, seals in far distance.

As if one world was not enough.
As if

Sanctuary was always further off,
And even the Island was not sure, or safe,

Beyond the shore, beneath the church, another.

Timeless.

Its clock
Ticks round in neaps, springs, weather, moons,
The flocks

That pause here in their tides, migrant between
One elsewhere and another. Small birds, knots,

Settle and unsettle,
Swerve and fall

Together, purposeful
As one heart, one

Single indrawn
Exhaled breath;

One truth.

Flickering within it,
Countless convergent

Streams, flights, currents
Fasten and unfasten –

Uncertainty, evasion,
The soft equivocation

Of mist, or rain.

Seals singing: Hooooo.

Who

Moans like the wind in an upturned keel on an autumn night
When a ship might crack her back on Manuel Heed,
Smashed to matchwood on the Ploo;

Who howls
And sings round Guile Point, Goul'stone, Parton Steel?

Like hounds on a line
Or wind in the wires
Or geese on the wing on the Slakes, or the cry of the wild
Wolves hungering under the sea,
Or women weeping;

Searching,
Seeking

From the Low to the Sandeel Beds, over Fenham Flats
To the Mill Burn, the Foolwork Burn, the Blacks,
And the Stinking Gut, to the sheer of the Old Law dunes
And out to the lea, to the shelter under the Farne,
To the Haven, the Fairway, the harbour, the safety zone
That can turn in the flick of a tail from a port in a storm
To a place of harm,
To a shoal, to a squall, to a wreck of a rock:

Who mourns,

Moaning, groaning, rising and falling, soft and low
Or nothing at all,
Like women weeping;

Like the sound of nothing at all;
Or women weeping?

Seals continue.

Out on the far Sand Rig or the Lang Batt,
They loll like slugs on the dry all day, ready to fight

Or mate, or to slip in an instant
From a lumbering sack of cockles, out of weight

Into a missile – deadly, graceful. Who

Are they, easing between known ground and the uncertain
Cold blue element, so almost human?

IV

	Cobwebs doon the lonnen,
Tick tock, tick tock,	*Mackerel*
Hurryin', scurryin',	*i' the sky,*
High wetter, low wetter,	*The dog afore*
Nivvor trust the weather, boys...	*it's maister,*
	Better watch the tide...

The tide is 'closed', the Island made perfect,
Spread out in its blue sea, a locked box, a casket

Of relics, jewels; a kist and a cradle.

Summer gulls, terns.

For him to whom the eider
Was daughter, the crinoid

His rosary, his cross
The cormorant's outstretched wings,

To pray was to listen.

The boat he travels in
Now a nailed box.

The oak that teemed with life,
Hewn; fixed with bees' wax.

Sea-salt, keep him safe
And bitumen preserve him

From rot; from time.

Church bell tolls.

*'Pagans from the Northern Regions came with a naval force to Britain like stinging
hornets and spread on all sides like fearful wolves... And they came to the church
of Lindisfarne; laid everything waste with grievous plundering, trampled the holy
places with polluted steps, dug up the altars and seized all the treasures of the holy
church. They killed some of the brothers, took some away with them in fetters; many
they drove out, naked and loaded with insults. Some they drowned in the sea.'*

(SIMEON OF DURHAM)

The mason has carved a stone.
Axes, swords,

Tell without words
What became of us. Fire,

Blood, tears. Prayer.
Flight our only answer,

The sands before us. Flight
As the goose before the wind.

Dunes, hiss of bent-grass.

At Green Shiel, the sun beats down
On the shapes of deserted houses,

On willow bush and fireweed
And the white grass of Parnassus,

On stones of byre and bedroom,
Hearths, hidden in bent-grass.

A doorway, a threshold, a beginning.
Here, snail and bunting

Have made their shelter. Peace
Is life, continuing

Oblivious, without us –
Our better selves, our children –

Here, in this hollow of ruins.

V

Sea: a single breaker.

Under the Priory, that stone crook
Bent like the frame of a sand-happed shipwreck,

Squat the shed-boats, strange, amphibian –
Black whales, hauled out; beached worlds flipped

Upside down, in a distant echo
Of all the ships that ever heaved their cargo

Onto the shore, half sea, half human.

166

A burst of rapid chatter from the nest.
Into the shadowed
Dark and tarry upturned boat-shed flits
A swallow.

Last month it was safe in the egg,
The egg secure in the nest,
The nest shrugged tight in the scarphed oak frames
Of the upturned wreck,

Its planks stiffened with sailcloth
And its sails with tar;
And heaped inside from gunwale to keel,
Anchors, rope, oars –

Woodworm and rust.
All the Island possessed.

Then out of the white egg, out
Of the nest, the cupped hands
Of the boat, beached, never to sail again,
Into the sun

And the wind's currents
Bursts – a bullet,
The blue of Africa on its wings,
In its bandit's mask, a red flash of desert,

Already burning in its skull,
A spelk of magnet.

Cold wind rush. Thin twitter of birds.

And the year turns. Sudden
Exposure. Cold. The seas

Pounding the North Shore,
Ice in the wind. Winter

Hacks the dunes, scours
Old walls, sandstone

Arches, the roofless
Vaults of the righteous,

Bows down the hawthorn
On the Crooked Lonnen.

From such storms fall
Goldcrest, fieldfare,

Exhausted, shivering,
The Isle their shiel, their shelter.

Tick tock, tick tock,
Summer in November,
Low wetter, high wetter,
Nivvor trust the weather, boys,
Hour-glass, weather-glass,
Nivvor beat a tide, lass,
Tick tock, tick tock,
Time runnin' oot.

The dog afore its maister,

Blue lowes i' the fire,

Black scum on the wetter,

Better watch the tide.

The Island is battening down. The castle, a snail,
Coils on its crag. Over the water at Beal

Barbed wire snakes in the sand, and a concrete pill-box
Squints from the bank at a cockeyed line of tank blocks.

In Goswick Sands, old iron rusts and ticks.

Far off, in a yawning sky, so blue it glares
Into its own mirage, surf's white fire
Flickers on a sandbar. Out of nowhere

Into nowhere, scream the fighter-jets.

Roar of RAF jets.

And down in the causeway's green fringes of weed
Tiny crabs like pieces of jewellery – buttons, beads,
Brooches, ear-rings – scuttle, dart and feed.

Here's one. A grey-green winkle
Scrambles on knuckles
And two pairs of stilettos.

A hand, hiding in a shell.

Goggle-eyed, it grapples
Weed, food, one pincer
Raised at a rival – a foil.

At once
Solitary and countless,

Tentative and furious,

A stone-age hermit, skulking in its cave,
The curve of its shear claw
Shielding its threshold,

Around it, its black bowl
Crusted with coiled white tube-worms,

Above it, the darkening sky, with stars, with questions.

Pink-footed geese flight cries.

VI

Miles away, in his bed, he heard them call

From the white wastes of the Arctic,
In his own heartbeat.

All day in the office,
Restless, their wings' rush.

So he jumped in his four-by-four
With a rucksack full of Gore-Tex,

His twelve-bore and his hip-flask,
And miles and hours later –

Full moon on the Swad.
Sleet showers. Cloud scud –

His gun-dog sniffing salt-grass,
Arrives at the Lang Brig End.

Now, into the Slakes,
Into the moonlight, into

His deeper self, he eases
As a seal returns to water.

Under night's camouflage
The widgeon's hush,

The pink-feets' slow paddle.
Before they call, he knows them.

The Black Low. The Mill Burn.
Step by step, that rhythm

Experience has taught him
To measure. He reads

The stones, the way the tide
Combs the grass, his compass.

And here they come, the geese –
Invisible, present

In their soft ink-ink, their wing-beats –
Incalculably ancient

And other-world, to settle
Soundless here. They slip

Between each indistinct
Element, lit

By the blue moon. His gun,
His total concentration,

Fixed on their flight, his weight –
Mud-shoes, gun-case,

Feet freezing to ice –
Anchoring him to the ooze,

He lifts, to the wind's scent,
Its sting of salt,

His whole self, in touch
With the world's heartbeat.

Single shot from a twelve-bore shotgun.

VII

Tick tock, tick tock,   *Cobwebs doon the lonnen,*
Hurryin', scurryin',
High wetter, low wetter,   *Blue lowes i' the fire,*
Spring come early,
Hour-glass, weather-glass,   *Black scum on the wetter,*
Berrellin', derrellin',
Tick tock, tick tock,   *Better watch the tide.*
Time runnin' oot.

Brent geese, quiet and far off, building in volume:

Slanting over the Sneuk, over
Goswick, that sky-writing, ominous, ancient
Far away, frightening, almost

Legible. Whose hand, whose voice
Whispers over vast distances, ice

Creaking in it, snow?

No one. But for miles at the tide's edge, geese –
Dark straggles of them – raise

Oaths, hymns, gutturals; and Fenham,
Stirring in its sleep,

In its own rank, spicy smells, its dribbles,
Its ooze, its salt-juices, its tidal creaks,

Opens itself to the sky, to the world, absorbs
Streams, strings of cells pouring

Down from nowhere into one dark body –
A rabble, a squabble, a whole hullabaloo
Trying to make sense of its singleness, an orchestra

Tuning its thousand primitive instruments,
Half bagpipe, half trumpet.

Loud hullabaloo of Brent geese ends.

And day breaks. On the mainland,
At Beal, from behind the Island,

Flooding the sands, the mud, as far
As Ross Beacons. At Fenham Le Moor

The narrow road runs down to the shore.

Footsteps up stairs to bird hide.

Balanced on this edge,
A kind of church; a refuge,

A place to be still, and listen.

All day they arrive at the Hide –
Wash in and leave – the retired

Insurance salesman from Hull,
The grandmother from Liverpool,

With their telescopes, tripods, flasks,
On their way to another place.

But another place is here

As the tide creeps in, a living
Breathing lung, its shallows

172

Flooding, slowly filling,
Draining again, its shadows

Lengthening, a place

Where hawthorn and robin
Meet face to face with salt-grass

And just as the season ripens
And turns, and again, the evening

Darkens, widgeon gather
Under the Mill, their voices

Carrying sky and winter
From long ago and farther

Than any road.
                    Now, you

Step out of your element. Listen.

Closer. In this moment
There is no one not a migrant

On his way to another place.

As the Island catches fire
In the sunset, and the mirror

Of the mudflats and the water
Returns it whole, desire

Catches you like the tide –
That longing to belong here,

That hunger for a likeness
Across so great a distance

No telescope can bridge it –

And flight its only answer.

VIII

Curlew, godwit,
Lapwing, plover,
On the run
Before the weather,

Brent goose, white wing,
Migrant, vagrant,
Bird of passage,
Traveller, emigrant,

Pilgrim, refugee,
Believer,
Fugitive,
Asylum-seeker.

Creeping, seeping,
Icy, salty,
Softly, slowly,
Tortuous, sinuous,

Winding, twining,
Bitter, briny,
Seeping, creeping,
Infiltrating,

Steeping and
Insinuating,
Drenching, drowning,
Inundating.

The wind dies down. The tide advances. All is still.
Out on the far sand rig, the seals

Raise their voices to the darkening sky.

Who are they singing to sleep with their lullabies?

Who? Who?

Seals: Hooooo.

I, Mark Bell,

Of Wooler Haugh Head, employed on the afternoon
Of September the fifth eighteen-hundred and one, conveying a gentleman

Onto the Island, turned for home, with another postilion
Over the sand, dark having not long fallen,

The coach creaking into the fog like our own funeral.

Who?

I, Tommy Foreman,

174

Butcher of Lowick in my blue-striped apron,
Bid ower-lang in the Northumberland Arms wi' Geordie Wilson,

Red nose, hot fire. One for the road? Why not, son. Soon
Cold in my liver, in my heart cold, cold in my marrow-bone,

My money-bag around my neck, an end-stone.

Who? Who?

I, Jean Bowes, who, with my husband,
Clicked off the lights and locked the door behind us

And headed in our purple Triumph Herald
Into the dark, the windscreen wipers waving

Goodbye, goodbye. We were looking forward
To Christmas, the holly berries blazed

Brightly over the mantelpiece. Before us lay
Rain, spray; the headlights useless, hard to find

The road, impossible. The car door slammed.

How cold your hand was, John, out on that sand.

My ticking watch, stopped at 3.30 a.m.

Creeping, seeping,   *Tick tock, tick tock,*
Icy, salty,   *Hurryin', scurryin',*
Softly, slowly,   *High wetter, low wetter,*
Tortuous, sinuous,   *Summer in November,*

Winding, twining,   *Berrellin', derrellin',*
Bitter, briny,   *Nivvor trust the weather, boys,*
Seeping, creeping,   *Low wetter, high wetter,*
Infiltrating,   *Tide flowin' harder,*

Steeping and   *Hour-glass, weather-glass,*
Insinuating,   *Nivvor beat a tide, lass,*
Drenching, drowning,   *Tick tock, tick tock,*
Inundating.   *Time runnin' oot.*

Actual recording: *'Hello, it's the Coastguard calling.*
Are you the people on Holy Island Causeway?'
'Yes we are. Yes. It's getting really high now.
Please just come now, please.
Come now.'

RAF Rescue Helicopter & radio: 'Steady... Steady...'
rises up occasionally through following:

I am in flight
From the spin, from the things that I know that I do not know,
From the crush, from the crowds, from the push, from the shove, from the street,
From the ice-age, from the heat-wave, from the fluttering heartbeat
At the core of it all; from the unseen hole
In the ozone's eye; from the fossil-fuel
In the soot-black, oil-rich mouth of the melting-pot.
From the permafrost.
From the drip, drip, drip
Of its shrinking ice; from the jumbo-jet;
From the stink, from the smoke, from the smog, from the slick
Of the gridlocked highways' car exhaust;
From the desert's breath, the glacier's roar,
From the sun's frank stare, from the climate police,
From the blazing forest, glimpsed from space,
From the rising tide, from the sea at our feet –
At our children's feet –
Send us an air-lift, a lifeboat, an ark –
Or at least

A refuge box.

Sound of feet on steps, door to Refuge Box, entering.

The latch clicks shut. A bench,
An opaque window.

The stench of piss. Fag ends.
A telephone on the wall.

Facing the incoming tide
Or the firing squad,

Or your own conscience,

Prisoner, when you lift
The telephone receiver

To your chill lips, whose number
Will you call?

Actual recording: *It's getting really high now.*
Please just come now, please.
Come now.'

IX

An hour before sunrise, sharp
Over the Island, the morning star
Pierces the first blue, and light flows.

Beneath the Refuge Box, the road
Emerges. First, the bridge. The Low
Seethes, its rip-tide spittle-flecked.

Slowly, the laminates part, pull back.
Behind their scalloped edge, the tarmac

Glitters; beside it, knotted coils
Of lugworm casts, and starry snails.

The tide sucks out. Not an even sheet
But a puzzle of pools. Its dazzling circuits
Fizz with froth and spawn, its brightness

Shimmering, the sky a race
Of shadows, tumbled brilliance
Streaming south, unstoppable.

The world is making itself again,
Piecing itself together, pinned

With spelks of glass and steely light.

The redshank, its beak
A sensitive pin-prick,

Feels worms, snails,
Twitch beneath it. Cities,

Pulsing, gorge on silt.
Across the mud-flats, cells,

Hungry for light, split,
Peel and multiply.

The road is a reef,
The mud beyond it, life

Teeming, prehistoric.

The Slakes are in flight.
Every species sweeps

Onward, or dives
Deeper into the mud,

Burning, bubbling
Back to its origins –

Unimagined plains,
Deserts, continents,

Conglomerates of grit,

Indecipherable
From endless rewriting.

Waders, quieter now.

Sand, sky and a flock
Of dunlin, shaken up.

Sediment in a glass.
They rise as one, and drift

Before the wind and tide
From mud-bank to sand-spit;

And scattered populations,
Blown like smoke, flow

Across earth's curve, to pick
Here, among the wreckage.

GLOSSARY

Glossary of Dialect and Unusual Words

Most of these words were used by Beadnell fishermen born in the early 20th century. I collected them throughout the 1990s, at a time when that generation was passing away, and the fishery which they represented was dwindling. The list is supplemented by additional words from Northumbrian farming communities, North-East 'Pitmatic' (coal-mining dialect), Border Scots dialect, and specialist vocabulary, as specified. Although many of the words in this list, or variations of them, are or were used throughout North-East England, and often in the Scottish Borders too, I have marked where I first or most often heard them, as follows:

A – Amble or Newbiggin; B – Beadnell; C – Craster; HI – Holy Island; P – Pitmatic (in these poems, East Durham); S – Seahouses; ST – South Tyne Valley; SV – specialist vocabulary; T – Tweedside; W – lead-mining terms collected in the Weardale/Allendale area. Those without attribution are in general use throughout North-East England.

aa'd-farrened: old-fashioned (B)

aback a: behind (B)

ablow: below (B)

aheight: high (B)

airt: direction (B)

ax: to ask (B)

back-end: autumn (B)

bagie: turnip (B)

bark-pot: an outdoor pot used to boil tannin-rich bark or 'cutch' to preserve fishing gear (SV)

barky: preserved with bark (B)

bastle: fortified Border farmhouse, ground floor used for livestock (SV)

batt: a small island (HI, T)

beadings: wooden strips to protect the overlapping joints of planks in a clinker-built boat (SV)

Beadlin: older inhabitants' pronunciation of Beadnell (B)

becket: loop of rope attached to pot (B)

bend: full flow (of the tide) (B)

bent: tied on (B)

benty: bents, bent-grass; also a place name in Beadnell (B)

berrel: to whirl (B)

bid: stayed (B)

bittled: beaten (B)

blaa': blow (B)

black barber: black frost (B)

blackjack: fully-grown coal-fish (B)

bleachin': lashing (of rain or snow) (B)

bleary: damp cold (B)

bleeze: blaze (B)

blether, blethor: chatter (T, B)

Bob Morrison: a traditional name for the grey heron among Tillmouth salmon netsmen (T)

boockies: whelks (B)

bool: to bowl, roll, bowl along, hurry (B)

boontree bush: elder bush (B)

born: a burn or stream (B)

bouse: lead ore in its rough state (W)

bowelt: graithing bolt, used to drag sea for lost fishing gear (B)

bows: buoys (B)

brae: to knock hard or hammer (B)

brailor: net on long pole for scooping fish aboard (B)

bratt: turbot (B)

brunt: burnt (B)

buddle: shallow vat in which lead ore is washed (W)

bus: seaweed-covered rock (B)

butt: flounder (C)

byennie: blenny (B)

byens: bones (B)

byeuts: boots (B)

caa': eddy, curl, turn (B, T)

caa'd: cold (B)

caa'driff: shiver (B)

caaldies: rats (taboo word) (B)

cairn net: net anchored by a heap of stones (T)

canch: stone in pit (P)

Candlish: John Candlish, 19th-century owner of glass and bottleworks at Seaham Harbour.

capin': placing stones upright on top of a drystone wall (ST)

carlin: space forward in coble, beside step for mast (B)

carr: a rock (B)

carra-paa'd: left-handed; clumsy (B)

Cars'well: Cresswell, a village on the Northumberland coast (A)

cauld: weir (T)

chum'uns: empty wagons (P)

claed: covered, clothed (B)

claes: clothes (B)

claggy: sticky (B)

clarty: muddy (B)

clash: gossip; throw (B)

clatter: chatter (B)

clecken: a brood (B)

cleek: to catch salmon using stick and hook (B, T)

cloots: rags (B)

cockle: clear one's throat (B)

coower: to cower or droop the head (B)

corbie craa': carrion crow

cord-rig: prehistoric cultivation banks of the kind found beneath Hadrian's Wall (SV)

cowble: Northumbrian coble (Beadnell pronunciation)

crack: talk (B)

cree: pigeon loft

creeve: crab or lobster pot (B)

creeve-stones, creeve-styens: stones used as weights in creeves (B)

crined: wizened, shrunken (B)

crook: one of the timbers which fan out forward in coble (B)

crowdie: oatmeal and water (T)

cruse: lively, energetic (B)

cuddy duck: eider duck (B)

cundy: drainage ditch (B)

danderin': wandering (B)

darse, darsay: dare say; an exclamation (B)

Deed Men: men working in lead mine in job that did not produce ore, e.g. driving levels (W)

deed tides: neap tides (B)

deeds: waste rock in lead mine (W)

derrel, durrel: to hurry (B)

dip: deep (B)

dishalagie: coltsfoot, locally butterbur (B)

divvilment: naughtiness (B)

dockens: dock leaves (B)

dog afore its maister: a rough sea which reaches land before the wind that caused it (S)

dogger: green crab (B)

dookas: large floats (B)

dopper: oilskin (B)

dowter: daughter (B)

draw-knife: a blade with a handle at each end used to remove large amounts of timber (SV)

drowt: one of the twin 'keels' on which a coble rests. See 'Scowbel'. (A)

drumly: clouded (B)

dub: a muddy pool (T)

durrellin': hurrying, speeding (B)

dyke: drystone wall; to build such a wall (B)

Egyncleugh: the deep rocky cleft ('cleugh') to the sea beneath the curtain wall of Dunstanburgh Castle

end-stone, end-styen: weight on end of a fleet of creeves (B)

esh: ash, ash tree (B)

ether: adder (B)

fagarrashin: mess, upheaval (B)

Fastworker: modern fibreglass inshore fishing boat, built for speed (SV)

fatther-lasher: sea-scorpion (B)

Featherblaa': highest dune in Beadnell Bay (B)

fest'ners: obstacles which snag nets (S)

fettle: to mend, put right (B)

filler: miner who fills wagons with loose coal underground (P)

fines: better quality lead ore (W)

finner: killer whale (B)

fishroom: space amidships in coble (B)

fit: fought (B)

flee: fly (B)

fool groond: rough ground (B)

forefoot: curved 'keel' extending half way aft from bows of coble (B)

fozy: spongy; rotten (B)

fresh: a spate (A)

frone: starfish (B)

galloways: pit ponies (P); also refers to a hardy breed of cattle (SV)

gey: very (B)

glaikit: clumsy (B)

glaur: sticky mud (B, T)

gliff: shock, fright (B)

glut: fish slime (T)

gob-stick: stick used by fishermen to remove swallowed hooks from fish (C, T)

gollerin': shouting (B)

gollup: to gobble (B)

gormer: cormorant (B)

graith: grade, kin, belonging (B)

greed: to covet (B)

gripe: narrowing of coble at forefoot, to grip the sea (B)

guddle: to catch salmon by hand (T)

guffies: pigs (taboo word) (B)

gump: same as 'guddle' (T)

gurrelly: rough, gloomy (B)

gut: path or opening, e.g. between rocks (B)

haa'd: hold (B)

haa'd your wheesht: be quiet (B, T)

haa'k: to sell from door to door (B)

hairt: heart (B)

Haliwerfolk: the people of St Cuthbert, i.e. those in County Durham and its Northumbrian Palatinate (SV)

hangy: dejected (ST)

happed: covered (B)

harl: barb or filament (SV)

harrin': herring (B)

hashy: rough, windy (B)

haugh: flat, boggy ground (B, T)

hawser: a small cable (SV)

haygellin': trundling, as of a barrow (B)

hemmel: cattle shed with arched entrance (B)

herrod: herd, shepherd (B)

heugh: a rocky outcrop on land, e.g. Hip's Heugh, Howick (B)

hind: contracted farm labourer (B); the 'Hinds' Hooses' are a landmark at Howick.

hingin's: twine attaching net to tow (A)

hinny: term of affection (B)

hobble: short seas (B)

hoolet: owl (B)

hootchin': heaving, teeming (B)

hoppin's: twine attaching net to tow (B)

horns: protuberance of gunwale either side of coble's stern (B)

hotchin' tub: machine used to sieve rough lead ore through water to extract finer ore (W)

howk: dig (B)

howway: come on!

hoy: throw (B)

hurpel: hobble (B)

hurrel: hurry (B)

hyem: home (B)

hyeuk: hook (B)

hyeutter: the barbed end of the hook (A)

hyeven: haven (B)

inwaver: inner supporting stringer in a coble (B)

Jack shine the lowe: children's name for the moon; also a children's game (B)

jaloose: figure out (B)

jeannies: spinning machines (T)

Jock Scott: this and the other names in this passage of *Tweed* are all types of salmon or trout fly (SV)

jud: a section of coalface to be taken down, as in 'to kerve a jud', to undercut a coalface (P)

keel: ruddle, ochre used to mark sheep (B, T)

kelpie: water demon (T)

kerve: to undercut coal (P)

kex: the dry stems of umbelliferous plants such as hogweed (B)

kibble: wooden or iron bucket used to carry lead ore to surface of mine (W)

kist: chest or trunk to hold belongings (B)

kittle: nervous; to tickle (B)

knowe: knoll (B)

kye: cattle

kyel: kale (B)

kyel-frone: sun starfish (B)

lade: watercourse (T, B)

laid-in: description of 'tumblehome' or inward curve of a coble's top planks (B) *leashin':* lashing (B)

level: horizontal drift made for mine access or drainage (SV)

lines: long lines, which carried up to 1,400 hooks for haddock and cod (B)

linn: waterfall (T)

linty: linnet (B)

lipper: white caps on sea (B)

Londonderry: powerful Anglo-Irish aristocratic family, who owned collieries on Durham coast

lonnen: path, lane

lough, low: lake (ST), water (HI)

lowes: flames, lights (B)

lowp: to leap (B)

lowse: loose, set free (B)

maa'n: must (B)

marks: landmarks, lined up for navigation (B)

mell: mallet (B)

mind: to remember (B)

morn' (the): tomorrow (B)

moss: bog (B)

mowldie: mole (B)

muckle: great, big (B)

mullymac: fulmar (B)

mushel: mussel (B)

musk-shells: cuttlefish (B)

naen: none, no (B)

nancies: squat lobsters (B)

neeve: fist (B)

nigh-handed: near (B)

norrard: north (B)

owertorned: overturned (B)

paddle-hoosh: lumpsucker (B)

pap-stoenes: soft coral, dead men's fingers (B)

patter: light conversation (B)

peel: fortified Border tower

pees'it: lapwing (B)

pellet: small float (B)

perrin: bobbin (B)

picket: boat hook (B)

pickie: tern (B)

pigs: moulds used in lead smelting to produce ingots (SV)

pike: small temporary haystack in a field (B)

piker: killer whale (A)

pillin: green crab when soft (B)

pilot: oystercatcher (B)

piner: penetrating cold south-easterly wind (B)

piper: spider crab (B)

pistil: lobster with no claws (B)

plantin: plantation (B)

plasher: porpoise or dolphin (B)

plowtin': pottering (B)

podler: small coal-fish (B)

Point: the peak moment when the incoming tide reaches a netting station on the Tweed (T)

poke: bag (B)

poother: powder; specifically gunpowder (B)

poss: to beat clothes in water with a stick to wash them

poy: boat stick (B)

prog: to prick (B)

putter: miner who conveys coal from the face to the flat (P)

ram plank: the bottom plank of a coble, the first to be laid down when it is built (SV)

rammel: small stones among coal, rubbish (P)

range: long seas (B)

rash: energetic (B)

rashers: rushes (B)

Reed Raa': Red Row, a village near Amble

reed up: clear up (B)

reek: smoke (B)

reivin': tearing, snatching (B)

rents: cracks which open as a wooden boat dries out (B)

rigg, rig: ridge

ripper: cross-pole carrying double hand-line (B)

rive: to tug or tear (B)

rocket house: shed where coastguard's rocket life-saving apparatus was kept (SV)

rouk: river mist (T)

rowells: rollers attached to side of coble (B)

rowelly: rough (B)

ruther: rudder (B)

saa'ted: salted (B)

sair: sore, hard, extreme (B)

sark: shirt (B)

scaa'din': burning cold (B)

scarph: to join wood to form a continuous piece (SV)

scoot: guillemot (B)

scorbels, scowbels: twin keels aft, on which coble rests (B)

scraffle: to scramble (B)

scraped (to have tongue scraped): to pretend more refined speech (B)

scumfish: to smother (B)

scut: top upper plank at coble's stern (B)

scut-iron: protective iron band along edge of scut (B)

sea-cat: cat fish (B)

sea-mice: small wading birds (B)

seg: sedge (B)

sewin' nail: copper nail fastened with 'rove' (rivet), used to 'sew' planks of coble together (B)

shaa': stalk (B)

shad: shallow place or bank (B)

shoon: shoes (T)

shoot: to set pots, nets or lines; also, to shout (B)

sicenlike: such like (B)

sixpenny-men: squat lobsters (HI)

skeer: outlying rock (B)

skeldy: porpoise (B)

skelp: slap (B)

skeyn: to shell, as of mussels for bait (B)

skowbs: sticks which have been cut for pot rails (B)

skyul: school (B)

slack: dip in ground; shallow valley; mud-flat; cessation of tide's flow (1st two ST, 3rd HI; 4th B)

slavver: bother (B)

slimes: residue in lead ore washing process (W)

smiddum: sludge of lead ore deposited when ore is washed, later collected for smelting (W)

smiddy: smithy (B)

smooth: sandy ground (B)

sneggle: to catch salmon by foul-hooking (T)

sneuk: rocky point, as at Seahouses and Holy Island (HI)

sneuk: to sniff about, as a dog (B)

sneyds: snoods, attaching hooks to lines (B)

sollan: gannet (B)

soocker: lamprey (B)

sorra: sir; now only in expression: 'sorra, haa'd yeer tongue!' (B)

sorrer: sorrow

spaa'n: spawn (B)

spar: crystal, such as fluorspar (W)

spelk: splinter (B)

spuggie: sparrow (B)

starkies: starlings (B)

starvin': withering cold (B)

steed: steading, home (B)

steel: rocky promontory, as in Boulmer Steel (C)

stem-post: outermost, upright timber running the length of a coble's bow (SV)

stife: smoke (B)

stoneman: miner employed to drive stone drifts or to cut away stone (P)

stoor: dust (B)

stowed oot: full up (B)

styen, stoene: stone (B)

sumpter: smelting pot (W)

swad: zostera, and area of mudflats where it grows (HI)

swatter: jellyfish (B)

sweel: swell (B)

sweels: swivels attaching buoy to pots (B)

swull: shallow basket used to hold long line (B)

tab: cigarette

tack hyeuk: place on either side of coble's bows to attach sail (B)

tacketty boots: hobnail boots (B, T)

taggarine-man: tinker (B)

tarree: arctic tern (C)

teamer: man who shovels coal from staithe onto ship; works with trimmer (SV)

teerum: tern (S)

thoft: thwart, seat in coble (B)

thoweld: thole pin for oars (B)

thropple: throat (B)

thruff-stone: tie stone in a drystone wall (ST)

thrussel: thistle (B)

tier: lot, used in derogatory expression 'aa' the tier' (all that e'er) (B)

timm'ers: timbers, oak 'frames' of a coble (B)

tiv: to (A)

tommy noddy: puffin (B)

toozled: tousled (B)

tows: ropes (B)

traal: trawl (B)

trammel: screen or sieve for lead ore (SV)

trapple: trample (B)

trimmer: man employed to level coals as they are loaded onto a ship (SV)

trink: dip in sand holding deeper water (B)

tuck: miller's thumb, scorpion fish (B)

tudelems: small seabirds, e.g. knots, dunlin (S)

tummel: fall (B)

tup: male sheep, to mate sheep

tyaen: taken (B)

tyed-legs: brittle-star (B)

varnigh: almost, very nearly (B)

waller: to waddle, move as a seal on land (B)

waregoose: barnacle goose (B)

wares: seaweed (B)

wesh: to wash (B)

wetter: water (B)

whin: gorse (B)

whinstone: basalt

whisht, wheesht: hush, quiet

whullicks: winkles (B)

whuppin's: fastenings, bindings (B)

wicket: small gate (B)

widder: widow

wittery-wagtail: pied wagtail (B)

wizenbank fair: extremely messy (B)

whumlick: hemlock and similar umbelliferous plants, such as hogweed (B)

wullymint: guillemot (B)

wund: wind (B)

yammer: to talk, whine (B)

yap: talk meaninglessly (B)

yark: to beat (B)

yeddle: liquid run-off from manure (ST)

yen: one (B)

yetlin: a three-toed iron pot (B)

yett: gate (T)

yowes: ewes

ACKNOWLEDGEMENTS

The Wund an' the Wetter, *Dunstanburgh* and *The Blue Lonnen* sequence have all been previously published in book form. To their publishers, Peter Mortimer (Iron Press), Andy Croft (Smokestack Books), and James and Catherine Dodds (Jardine Press), I owe great thanks. Thanks also to the Northumbrian Language Society and the anonymous donor who made possible the publication of *The Wund an' the Wetter*, and to Robert Leach at Selkirk Lapwing Press for publishing *This Far and No Further*, *Two Countries* and *An Ill Wind* in the chapbook *Seven Silences* (2007).

Some of these poems, or extracts from them, have appeared in anthologies, including: *Atoms of Delight* (pocketbooks, 2000), *Staying Alive* (Bloodaxe Books, 2002), *Fields of Fire* (Quita, 2002), *The Thunder Mutters* (Faber, 2005), *Tweed Rivers* (platform projects and Luath Press, 2005), *North by North-East* (Iron Press, 2006), *Writing on the Wall* (Arts UK, 2006), *Both Sides of Hadrian's Wall* (Selkirk Lapwing Press, 2006), *Pendulum – the poetry of dreams* (Avalanche, 2008), *Women's Work* (Seren, 2008), *No Space But Their Own* (Grey Hen Press, 2010), *Not Only the Dark* (WordAid, 2011), *Entanglements* (Two Ravens Press, 2012) and *Running Before the Wind* (Grey Hen Press, 2013). Poems, or extracts, have appeared in art books, including *Northern Exposures* (Chris Steele-Perkins, Northumbria University Press, 2007) and *James Dodds: Tide Lines* (Ian Collins, Studio Fine Arts, 2011). They have also appeared in a variety of newspapers, magazines and online magazines, including: *News from Hadrian's Wall*, *Red Herring*, *The Times Literary Supplement*, *The Guardian*, *The Daily Telegraph*, *The Journal*, *Markings*, *Revival*, *Coastal Views*, *International Notebook of Poetry*, *Iota* and *The Clearing*. *Borderers* is recorded on the CD *Lecchemede* by Andrew and Margaret Watchorn (Andrew also provided artwork for previous publications), and *Coble Counting Song* is set and sung by Jim Mageean on his CD *Gan Canny*. *The Pigeon Men* was broadcast on *Flog It* on BBC 2 TV. *The Refuge Box* was shortlisted for a Maritime Media Award in 2008, and is used in Dansformation's performance, *Northumbriana*.

Too many people have supported my work to name them. I am indebted to every one of them, and particularly to all the organisations and individuals who commissioned poems, including all those named in the introduction, Steve Chettle (Arts UK), Steve Cowton and Alnwick Playhouse Trust, Graeme Rigby, photographer Nigel Shuttleworth, Adam Sutherland, James Carter and Tweed Rivers

Interpretation Project, Scottish Borders Council, and Bamburgh and Easington Colliery Parish Councils. Huge thanks to everyone who contributed voices or sounds to the recordings, including Trevor Fox, Tom Goodman-Hill, sound artist Chris Watson, the late Carlotta Johnson and all who joined us at NE1 FM, Margaret Ayden and Seahouses First School, and Slate Hall Riding Centre, Seahouses. Particular thanks to the BBC producers who have commissioned poems, or used them imaginatively in their work, including Tim Dee, Sara Davies, Adam Fowler, Benjamin Chesterton, Geoff Bird, Rebecca Nicholson and Elizabeth Allard. Thanks most of all to poet and producer Julian May, a tremendous ally, without whom several of these long poems would not exist.

I am grateful also to the following: to all those who have read and commented on the poems, especially Nicholas Baumfield, Chris Preddle and Martin Pacey; to Ken Cockburn at platform projects for editing the first version of Tweed; to all the musicians with whom I've performed, especially Chris Ormston and Alistair Anderson; and to all the artists with whom I have collaborated, especially James Dodds; to all the poets and poetry event organisers – too many to list – who have invited me to perform work, and to all my friends who have helped with research, walked with me, brought my work to a wider audience, or simply inspired me. Particular thanks to Dr Keith Armstrong, Harry Beamish, Sue Clifford and Angela King at Common Ground, Mark Cocker and all at New Networks for Nature, Olivia Lomenech Gill, Mary and Stuart Manley of Barter Books, Alnwick; and most of all to Neil Astley and everyone at Bloodaxe Books.

Special thanks to the many people I interviewed: along Hadrian's Wall, on the Northumberland and Durham coast, along the Tweed, on Holy Island and elsewhere; particularly the farming, fishing, boat-building and mining families who gave their time and shared their experiences, often at very difficult moments. Without them, these poems could not have been written.

I am grateful for financial support during the writing of some of this work from the Arts Foundation, Northumberland Coast AONB Partnership and Arts Council England. Lastly, thanks to my parents – loving, generous, forbearing, and sometimes accidental, patrons of the arts. This book is dedicated to them.

Printed in the USA
CPSIA information can be obtained
at www.ICGtesting.com
JSHW012016140824
68134JS00025B/2450